RULES

OF

WEALTH

PEARSON

At Pearson, we believe in learning – all kinds of learning for all kinds of people. Whether it's at home, in the classroom or in the workplace, learning is the key to improving our life chances.

That's why we're working with leading authors to bring you the latest thinking and best practices, so you can get better at the things that are important to you. You can learn on the page or on the move, and with content that's always crafted to help you understand quickly and apply what you've learned.

If you want to upgrade your personal skills or accelerate your career, become a more effective leader or more powerful communicator, discover new opportunities or simply find more inspiration, we can help you make progress in your work and life.

Pearson is the world's leading learning company. Our portfolio includes the Financial Times and our education business, Pearson International.

Every day our work helps learning flourish, and wherever learning flourishes, so do people.

To learn more, please visit us at **www.pearson.com/uk**

THE
RULES
OF
WEALTH

A personal code for
prosperity and plenty

RICHARD TEMPLAR

PEARSON

Harlow, England • London • New York • Boston • San Francisco • Toronto • Sydney
Auckland • Singapore • Hong Kong • Tokyo • Seoul • Taipei • New Delhi
Cape Town • São Paulo • Mexico City • Madrid • Amsterdam • Munich • Paris • Milan

PEARSON EDUCATION LIMITED
Edinburgh Gate
Harlow CM20 2JE
Tel: +44 (0)1279 623623
Fax: +44 (0)1279 431059
Website: www.pearson.com/uk

First published 2007 (print)
Second edition published 2012 (print and electronic)
Third edition published 2013 (print)
This edition published 2015 (print and electronic)

© Richard Templar 2007 (print)
© Richard Templar and Pearson Education Limited 2012 (print and electronic),
2013 (print)
© Richard Templar 2015 (print and electronic)

Pearson Education is not responsible for the content of third-party internet sites.

ISBN: 978-1-292-08643-9 (print)
      978-1-292-08645-3 (PDF)
      978-1-292-08646-0 (ePub)
      978-1-292-08644-6 (eText)

British Library Cataloguing-in-Publication Data
A catalogue record for the print edition is available from the British Library

Library of Congress Cataloging-in-Publication Data
A catalog record for the print edition is available from the Library of Congress

10 9 8 7 6 5 4 3 2 1
19 18 17 16 15

Cover design by Nick Redeyoff

Print edition typeset in 10.5/12pt ITC Berkeley Oldstyle Std by 71
Print edition printed and bound in Great Britain by Clays Ltd, Bungay, Suffolk

NOTE THAT ANY PAGE CROSS REFERENCES REFER TO THE PRINT EDITION

Contents

Introduction

There's an old saying 'Money, money, money – it's all they can think about'. Unlikely to be true of course, given that hardly anybody thinks about money itself (unless they happen to be a coin collector). The reason we all pursue and desire and fiercely protect money is because of what we can do with it.

And no, of course money can't buy you love or happiness. Although it can buy a good deal of pleasure – and remove a lot of unhappiness. But it can buy you plenty of other things. Over the years I've identified the ten things which people most seem to want to spend their money on:

1 **Security**. A home of your own and enough money in the bank to support you in the way you want, plus a bit in hand for emergencies, and a big enough pension to ensure a comfortable retirement.

2 **Comfort**. A warm and spacious house, a big car, someone to clean or mow the lawns or do the laundry or mind the kids, and good quality medical care whenever you want it.

3 **Luxuries**. Exotic holidays, fine wines, meals in top-class restaurants, expensive clothes, the best seats at sports events or opera or whatever you enjoy.

4 **Mobility**. First-class train seats and plane tickets, trips on cruise ships, and chauffeur-driven cars wherever you are in the world.

5 **Status**. Prestigious invitations, access to important people and exclusive clubs, and perhaps even gratifying deference from others.

6 **Influence**. As a generous donor of substantial sums, being able to make sure that your views and wishes are listened to and taken seriously.

7 **Freedom**. Not being dependent on employers, bosses, creditors, clients, customers. Not being a slave to the calendar, diary or clock. Knowing you won't have to be a burden on your children.

8 **Leisure**. Time to do the things you want, go where you want, meet who you want, when you want.

9 **Popularity**. Being able to entertain friends, acquaintances and contacts frequently and generously, which does wonders for your social life.

10 **Philanthropy**. Being able to make regular and substantial donations, which gives you the satisfaction of helping people, supporting organizations and furthering causes you believe in.

Seems a reasonable enough list to me. And whether it's some or all of those things that you'd like more of, you'll need to know how to go about generating greater wealth – which means you need to know what it is that separates the wealthy from the not-so-wealthy. So, what you need to know is what principles, and what behaviours the rich have, that you don't (yet). Some of them you will realize that you know, but don't do. None of this is actually rocket science, it's about understanding and then doing. I've studied a lot of wealthy people and it's clear to me that there are some fundamental common principles followed by almost all. The bulk of the Rules in this book fall into that category. Then there are also some principles which some rich people swear by, but not all. I've included some of those too for good measure, just in case you too are one of the people they do the trick for.

Security, comfort, luxuries, mobility, status, influence, freedom, leisure, popularity, philanthropy – that's all some people think about. They may not be everything, they may not even guarantee a happy life, but they're a pretty good basis to build happiness on.

I've tried to set out in this book the most important Rules that will help you achieve these ten things. All of them purport to be about accumulating money, and of course in a sense they are, but at heart they're about money only as a means to an end. A means to achieve those ten ends.

Of course I don't claim that these hundred or so Rules are the only means to these particular ends. You may encounter others along the way that you find helpful. If so, please do feel free to share them. You can post your very own Rules on my Facebook page at www.facebook.com/richardtemplar

Richard Templar

Acknowledgements

I would like to thank Dan Clayden, director of Clayden Associates – Independent Financial Advisers (www.claydenassociates.co.uk) who was so kind as to go through a draft of this book in the early stages and put me right on a few things and is one of the best financial advisers I have ever met professionally.

I would also like to dedicate this book to my delightful father-in-law who manages his money in a kind, generous, honest and moral way and still manages to make it work for him efficiently and expertly. He is an example to all of us. He is a Rules Player par excellence.

THINKING
WEALTHY

Money is a concept. You can't really see or touch it (unless you are holding a gold bar in your hand). You can only do that with some physical symbol of it like bank notes or a cheque. Bits of paper, yes, but bits of paper with enormous power.

The concept of money comes with a lot of baggage to most of us. We have an inherent belief that it is good or bad and that wanting it is good or bad. That loving it is good or bad. That spending it is good or bad.

What I am going to suggest in the first few Rules is that maybe, just maybe, how we think about wealth might be holding us back from having wealth. If, in our heart, we believe (even subconsciously) that money is a bad thing and having lots and lots of it is a really bad thing, then chances are we might be undermining our own efforts, unwittingly, to get lots of it.

I am also going to get you to look at how much effort you are prepared to put into making money. It's a bit like a sport – the more you practise the better you become. Likewise you can't make money while being lazy. You've got to put in some work here, you know.

You've also got to know pretty intimately what you want, why you want it, how you think you are going to get it, what you are going to do with it after you've got it – stuff like that. No one said this was going to be easy . . .

RULE 1

Anybody can be wealthy – you just need to apply yourself

The lovely thing about money is that it really doesn't discriminate. It doesn't care what colour or race you are, what class you are, what your parents did, or even who you *think* you are. Each and every day starts with a clean slate so that no matter what you did yesterday, today begins anew and you have the same rights and opportunities as everyone else to take as much as you want. The only thing that can hold you back is yourself and your own money myths (see Rule 7).

> ## YOU HAVE THE SAME RIGHTS AND OPPORTUNITIES AS EVERYONE ELSE TO TAKE AS MUCH AS YOU WANT

Of the wealth of the world each has as much as they take. What else could make sense? There is no way money can know who is handling it, what their qualifications are, what ambitions they have or what class they belong to. Money has no ears or eyes or senses. It is inert, inanimate, impassive. It hasn't a clue. It is there to be used and spent, saved and invested, fought over, seduced with and worked for. It has no discriminatory apparatus so it can't judge whether you are 'worthy' or not.

I have watched a lot of extremely wealthy people and the one thing they all have in common is that they have nothing in common – apart from all being Rules Players of course. The wealthy are a diverse band of people – the least likely can be loaded. They vary from the genteel to the uncouth, the savvy to the plain stupid, the deserving to the undeserving. But each and every one of them has stepped up and said, 'Yes please, I want some of that'. And the poor are the ones saying, 'No thank you, not for me, I am not worthy. I am not deserving enough. I couldn't. I mustn't. I shouldn't'.

That's what this book is about, challenging your perceptions of money and the wealthy. We all assume the poor are poor because of circumstances, their background, their upbringing, their nurture. But if you have the means to buy a book such as this and live in comparative security and comfort in the world then you too have the power to be wealthy. It may be hard. It may be tough but it is doable. And that is Rule 1 – anyone can be wealthy, you just need to apply yourself. All the other Rules are about that application.

RULE 2

Decide on your definition of wealth

So, what, to *you*, is wealth? This is one you have to sit down and work out in advance if you are going to get wealthy. My observation is that wealthy people invariably have worked this one out. They know exactly what, to them, wealth means.

I have a wealthy and extremely generous friend who says that he knew long ago when he was starting out in business that he would consider he had made enough when he wasn't living off the money he had amassed (which we will call his capital). Nor would he be living off the interest on his capital. No, he would consider himself wealthy when he was living on the interest on the interest on his capital. Sounds good to me.

Now, this friend knows how much his interest on the interest is making him, pretty much by the hour. Thus if we all go out for a meal in the evening he knows (a) how much the meal has cost and (b) how much he has made while eating the meal. He says that as long as (b) is more than (a), then he is happy.

This is setting the definition of wealth pretty high, you might think. Maybe you wouldn't want to set it this high. And that's fine of course. Then again, maybe you'd want to put some kind of figure on it. In the old days everyone wanted to be a millionaire. That was an easy one to judge if you'd got there or not. Today there are a lot of people who have houses worth more than that and they wouldn't consider themselves wealthy at all and yet haven't quite got around to upping the ante to wishing themselves billionaires.*

---

* Sorry, but to me a billion is a million million and I won't be persuaded otherwise.

My own definition, for comparison, is having enough so that I don't have to worry about having enough. How much is that? I never know. There always seems to be more to worry about – and less coming in. But seriously, I feel that I have been 'comfortable' since I started counting in thousands rather than in pounds. I know to the nearest thousand how much I've got, how much I need and how much I can spend.

For some people, not worrying might mean having enough to pay for any emergency that might arise in their family or home. So how will you define it? By the number of cars you own? Servants? Cash in the bank? Value of your house? Portfolio of investments? There are, of course, no right or wrong answers, but I do feel that until you've worked this one out you shouldn't read on. If we don't have a target we can't take aim. If we don't have a destination we can't leave home or we'll be driving around in circles for hours. If we don't have a definition how can we monitor or judge success? If we don't do this how will you know if this book has been helpful to you?

> **IF WE DON'T HAVE A DEFINITION HOW CAN WE MONITOR OR JUDGE SUCCESS? IF WE DON'T DO THIS HOW WILL YOU KNOW IF THIS BOOK HAS BEEN HELPFUL TO YOU?**

Set your objectives

By defining what you mean by wealth, you now have a destination. Setting your objectives is establishing a timetable to reach that destination. It's quite simple. If you know you are going to drive to a certain place it makes sense to know:

- what time you are leaving home

- what time you expect to arrive

- what route you are going to take

- what you will be doing when you get there.

Getting rich is exactly the same. You will want to know in advance what rich means to you, how you intend getting there, how long you expect it to take and what you are going to be able to do or want to do with your money when you get it.

So, having defined what wealth means to you, can you now see the importance of setting your objective? Think about how you intend getting rich and how long it is going to take you and then set your objective. It might be simple: 'I am going to be a millionaire by my fortieth birthday and I shall make my money by running my own property development company.'

That was easy. Well it was for me because I'm only making up an example for you. For you I wager it's going to be pretty hard. This is because you won't have thought about this before. Oh, I daresay you might have had a casual dream – I want to be very, very rich and/or famous and/or successful. But few people – only the rich, famous and successful ones in my observation – actually decide what and when and how. You have to if you too want to be wealthy. And I assume you do or you wouldn't be reading this far. Good for you.

Now set your objective. I can wait.

Back already? How did you get on? Your objective has to be realistic, honest and achievable. By realistic I mean that setting an objective of being the richest person in the world might happen but it isn't going to, it isn't realistic.

Honest means you have to be true to yourself and set an objective that you can live with and work with. Lying to yourself means it will fail. Lying to others means it will fail.

Achievable? Yes that too. If you know nothing about property and aren't interested in learning, have no capital and can't get a mortgage, then setting an objective to be a property developer isn't realistic, honest or achievable.

Happy with what you've got? Good. If not, have another bash at it and let's get a move on: we want to get you up and running as soon as possible.

> **YOU WILL WANT TO KNOW IN ADVANCE WHAT RICH MEANS TO YOU, HOW YOU INTEND GETTING THERE AND HOW LONG YOU EXPECT IT TO TAKE**

RULE 4

Keep it under your hat

Now you have embarked on a new journey, a new direction, it might be worth keeping it under your hat. There may come a time when you will need to discuss what you are doing with money mentors (see Rule 71) but for the moment don't broadcast what you are doing. There are several reasons for this:

- Other people's opinions can often be negative and this can put you off.

- If everyone is doing it, there may be less room for you.

- There's no need to give away all your best ideas.

- Having other people discussing your business among themselves is never good for you.

- You don't want to be seen as preaching or trying to convert people to your way of thinking.

- No one else really wants to know what you're up to – if they ask how you are, reply with a simple 'Fine' rather than a lengthy explanation of what you are doing.

- It's nice having a secret – it gives you a warm, smug, glowing feeling.

If you go round broadcasting what you're doing, there will be people around you who will get jealous and will do pretty well anything to put you off. After all, you are saying goodbye to them in a way. You are proclaiming that the old you, the old lifestyle, isn't good enough any more and you are off to pastures new. Of course they are going to be unhappy about that. So keep it under your hat. That doesn't cost anything or require you to do anything.

> **NOW YOU HAVE EMBARKED ON A NEW JOURNEY, A NEW DIRECTION, IT MIGHT BE WORTH KEEPING IT UNDER YOUR HAT**

Let this be our little secret. Carry on learning and practising the Rules but just don't go telling all and sundry – no matter how much you think they might benefit from reading this book. Leave a copy around by all means of course.

The interesting bit is that even if you did go telling everyone, they're unlikely to do anything about it. Most people would rather watch television than drag themselves out of their pit of poverty. I am only thinking of you when I say keep it under your hat. Anyone who gets religion of any sort needs to keep a tight lip on it. People really hate being preached at, lectured at, encouraged to think about their lifestyle or told that what they are doing isn't good enough. Gaining prosperity is one of those things you do privately, clandestinely, surreptitiously. Not that there is anything wrong, just that it's best done alone.

Most people are too lazy to be wealthy

You have to get up early, work hard all day and go to bed still working on your objective. Yes, money *does* sometimes grow on trees – or so it seems. Yes, people *do* win the lottery, the jackpot, the big prize. People *do* get sudden inheritances from long lost relatives. Yes, people *do* suddenly find fame and fortune where they sought for none. But it isn't going to happen to you. Well, the odds are that it won't. If you set your objective as 'Win the lottery and live in the lap of luxury for evermore', then read no further. Put this book down and go and buy lottery tickets. If your objective is a little more realistic then read on.

Most people are too lazy to be rich. They may say they want to be, but they don't. They may buy a lottery ticket as a sort of half-hearted gesture of wanting to be rich, but they aren't prepared to put in the work. They aren't prepared to make sacrifices, study, learn, work their socks off, put in the effort and make it a determined and concentrated focus of their life.

> **MOST PEOPLE ARE TOO LAZY TO BE RICH. THEY MAY SAY THEY WANT TO BE, BUT THEY DON'T**

And for a lot of them – not you – it is because they believe that if you do so you are somehow tainted with evil (see Rule 7). But is it OK to work hard to make money? Is it a worthwhile thing to want? It depends on why and what you are going to do with it I guess.

Most people don't want to do the work. Yes, they want the money but only if it comes to them by accident, by luck, by chance. Then it's OK. Then it's not tainted with sweat and work and passion and focus.

I think if you look at anyone rich enough to be a role model – Bill Gates, Richard Branson, Alan Sugar, Warren Buffett, Simon Cowell, James Dyson, Petr Kellner* – you'll notice only one thing in common…they work their socks off. They might make their money from computers, sales, business, the film industry, vacuum cleaners, pop music, radio stations, whatever. But the one thing they all share is the ability to do more in a day than most of us do in a month.

And that's the wonderful thing about wealth – it's lying around waiting to be claimed (remember Rule 1). And those who claim it are the ones who get up early, work hard and put in the hours.

And you are going to have to as well. I don't have loungers, weight shifters or decorative spongers on my team. I want hard-working, dedicated, focused, ambitious, driven money makers. With a sense of fun of course.

---

* I did have a bet with myself that you wouldn't have heard of him – the Czech Republic's first billionaire.

RULE 6

Get a reality check

It's amazing how many people just ignore the obvious. Especially poor people. No I'm not being prejudiced, I'm saying that this is part of the reason they're poor.* Some people moan a lot about not having enough, they make loads of excuses, they may work, but not hard enough or not in the right ways, and they hope that their problems will simply go away.

Well guess what? They won't go away. They're more likely to get worse. If you're struggling financially and wondering how to make more money – a lot or just a little – for those things that matter to you, you need to take positive action. Because I promise you that short of winning the lottery, nothing's going to change unless you do.**

So sit down and think constructively about what you can do to increase your wealth. And then do it. Nothing else will dig you out of the financial morass. Be realistic – about where you're going, what you're spending, what you're saving, and what you can do to set yourself on a new and more prosperous path.

**NOTHING'S GOING TO
CHANGE UNLESS YOU DO**

---

* I'm not talking about people starving in third world countries here – I'm talking about people with friends and neighbours who have more than them.
** And you can start by saving the cost of that lottery ticket every week. How much have you spent in your life on lottery tickets? Go on – work it out. And what have you won? That balance isn't going to change, you know – you're just throwing money down the drain. Take it from me, you won't win the jackpot.

This applies to saving money as well. If you want £20,000 in five years' time, it's no good putting away a fiver a month. You'll be lucky to save £1000 at that rate. If you want to save a specific amount of money, you need to work out exactly how much you need to save per week or month to do it. If it's not going to add up, don't bury your head in the sand. Work out how to save more, or extend your deadline.

If you know you have money vices, then face them. If you always spend £100 a month on beer, gadgets, shoes, whatever, then it's no good pretending that you don't when you make those financial plans. And if you know you struggle to save anything, there's no point pretending that you can suddenly put away £100 a month, every month.

I know it's very tempting to avoid looking at problems and disappointments, but if you do that you'll never get wealthy. If you're serious about making money, you have to start by finding the courage to confront the financial nasties in your life and do something about them.

RULE 7

Understand your money beliefs and where they come from

We all grow up with money myths. We get a lot of them from our parents and the way they bring us up. I can still hear my mother saying, 'A penny saved is a penny found', and to this day I still have no idea what it means. Maybe I'm lucky. My money myths are based on a lot of nonsense like that. But most of us have the following ingrained beliefs:

- Money is the root of all evil.*

- Money is dirty.

- I don't deserve to be rich.

- Money is only made by the greedy and dishonest.

- Money corrupts.

- You mustn't brag about money – never say how much you earn, are worth or paid for something (unless it is a bargain).

- You can't have money and be 'spiritually pure'.**

- You lose your friends if you get rich.

- You have to work too hard to get rich (see Rule 5).

- Happiness and money make poor bedfellows.

- The more you have, the more you'll want.

---

* It is actually the *love* of money that is supposed to be the root of all evil but is it a belief of yours?
** Whatever that means.

- It is somehow better to be poor.

- I wasn't meant to be rich – if I was I would have been by now.

- I'm not the right type to be rich.

Have a quick look through. Check which ones you believe. Check which ones strike a chord with you. Now you have to do a bit of that old-fashioned hard work. Write down ones that mean something to you. Add ones I've missed – there will be a few. Now work out why you hold these beliefs. Is it something you have actively thought about, reasoned out, dedicated some research to? Or are they inherited, left over, picked up along the way?

Get rid of any that you can question and accept are nonsense. Discard any that simply aren't true. And chuck out any that stand in the way, hold you back, stop you making some money.

What you should be left with is none at all, nothing, a blank sheet. Now you can write new beliefs such as:

- Money is OK.

- Wanting money is OK.

- I am going to be wealthy.

- I am prepared to put in the work.

Wealthy people have none of the troublesome money myths we poorer people have. They have purged them or never had them. If we too purge them, we stand a better chance of getting rich.

> # GET RID OF ANY BELIEFS THAT YOU CAN QUESTION AND ACCEPT ARE NONSENSE

Understand that wealth is a consequence, not a reward*

If you work hard at making money, you stand a better chance of becoming rich. You have to accept that money is a payment given to you for clever thinking and hard work. The harder and smarter you work, the more you will earn. You don't get given the money by a committee who examine whether you deserve it or not, whether you have been good enough or not. It is a direct consequence.

We often look at someone who has money and make all sorts of value judgements about whether they deserve it or not. We all do it. I was reading about Calvin Ayre – the internet bookie – who has grown very rich indeed running online gambling. He has something like 16 million customers in the US. The US Department of Justice isn't very happy about this and want to shut him down. Ayre isn't a US citizen and doesn't reside there. You can read all about him on the www.Forbes.com website (home of the really wealthy folk). If it isn't your home page it jolly well ought to be. You are in this to be wealthy, which means understanding where wealth comes from.

Back to Ayre. He has grown rich exploiting an alleged US law loophole whereby what he does is alleged to be illegal but he isn't in the country to commit any crime. Do we judge him? I don't. I study this information to see if I could make use of it. What might be wrong is the gambling. But I am aware that his consequence of hard work has been lots of money.

---

* I use the word 'reward' in the sense of a prize or bonus, not as a payment or renumeration.

I was watching a TV programme the other day about a chap who cleans and polishes cars for rich celebs and such like. He charges £5000 for car washing. Mind you, this does include polishing. Now, is his money a reward or a consequence? I don't think he would see it as a reward. It's the price he sets, and customers pay him because he is the best car cleaner in the world. The consequence of his business idea, skill and effort is to be very well paid.

> **YOU DON'T GET GIVEN THE MONEY BY A COMMITTEE WHO EXAMINE WHETHER YOU DESERVE IT OR NOT**

Decide what you want money for

This is part of your defining, setting an objective process. There are no right or wrong answers. For example, making a fortune and spending it all on cocaine seems, to me, like a foolish thing to do. But that's personal. You might find a problem with me spending mine on a decent Châteauneuf-du-Pape. We all spend on what we think will satisfy us, make us happy. We all choose our own pleasures and it's not for me to sit in judgement on anyone else.

So why do you want to be wealthy? The answers you give will tell you a whole lot about your hidden money myths and how you really see money.

> ## WE ALL SPEND ON WHAT WE THINK WILL SATISFY US, MAKE US HAPPY

Sometimes it's very simple: we have a dream and need the money to fulfil it. The dream comes first. Gerald Durrell had wanted a zoo since he was a small boy and wrote 36 bestselling books which helped to fund his zoo (on the island of Jersey). What's your dream?

It might not be that simple, however. I asked a close acquaintance why she wanted to be wealthier the other day and the results were quite revealing. She said she wanted to be 'better off' so that she could give her children more. And in giving them more, they would stay at home longer. And if they stayed at home longer, she wouldn't have to face a possible old age alone. So basically she wants to be wealthy to stave off loneliness.

Another acquaintance said he wanted to get wealthy so he could have adventures. When pressed further it seemed his adventures were the 'running away' sort where he could be young, free and single again.

Is money really the answer for either of these people? Is it for you?

When you know what you want greater wealth for, think also about alternative ways to meet your needs: I said earlier some people want to be wealthy so they can pay for medical care for any close family member that might need it. They could invest in some simple medical insurance to cover that instead.

Consider also what you *don't* need more money for. I like my toys – cars and boats – but have found that my investments in such things hasn't increased as my income has gone up. I still like old cheap sports cars and old boats that need plenty of maintenance. Do you really need as much as you think? If so, fine, you just need to be sure and be clear about it.

So what's your excuse? What do you want money for? It might be to free you from having a job, or it might not even be for yourself but to support causes you believe in. Set your own agenda, my friend, and keep it to yourself. But I do recommend you write it down, because it makes it so much more real. It is a useful exercise to look back on one day and see if your dream and achievements match.

RULE 10

Understand that money begets money

There is no greater truth than this – money makes money. It likes clustering together. It breeds quietly and quickly like rabbits. It prefers to hang out in big groups. Money makes money. The rich get richer; the poor get poorer. That's life. Yes, it is sad. But it does seem to be a fact. Now we can work hard ourselves and do something about it or we can sit around moaning and become part of the problem. The choice, as always, is entirely yours.

> ## MONEY MAKES MONEY.
> ## THE RICH GET RICHER

If you do want to do something about it, then it seems to make sense to me to make a tidy sum and use your money wisely to help the less fortunate than you. Or do whatever with it you so choose.

Once you have some money you'll be astonished at how quickly it can grow. I recommend you understand and learn the concept of compound interest as quickly as possible. And no, I am not going to tell you anything about it except it's vitally important that you know about it and make it a cornerstone in your building of wealth. The reason I'm not going to tell you anything about it is, firstly, this isn't that sort of a book and, secondly, I'm not going to do all the work for you.* That would be too easy and you'd learn

---

* Go and read *The Financial Times Guide to Investing* by Glen Arnold (Pearson Education, 2010).

nothing. My observation is that wealthy people get the idea of compound interest and the rest of us don't.

If you spend all you get, then this Rule will never work for you; it'll never get your money working for you. You have to set aside money for breeding purposes. If you ran a rabbit farm and killed and ate all your rabbits, you wouldn't have any left to keep going. Forget the rabbit farm – you're going to start a money farm. Your money will breed. You can then reinvest some and spend some – but you can't spend it all or you'll have no more rabbits. Look, this stuff isn't rocket science but it is amazing how many people simply don't get it. But you do now. You have been given the best tip I can give you.

- Put some money aside for breeding purposes.

- Cream a little off for spending.

- Reinvest the bulk to build up a good and healthy stock.

- Keep it to yourself.

Calculate the net return

Now doesn't *that* sound boring: 'calculate the net return'. Well it shouldn't be boring. Remember, this is about deciding if and when you're going to get that house or that holiday, when you can afford to give up work, how much you can leave to your kids or give to good causes, what kind of car you're going to drive. That's not boring. And the answer to when it's all going to happen will be affected by whether or not you calculate the net return.

You understand what 'net' means of course. But do you remember to factor in the costs, expenses, charges and tax before deciding whether to make an investment? For example, suppose you're tempted by a rate of 3 per cent. That might sound like a pretty good investment. But if you're a 40 per cent tax payer that's going to drop to a 'net' return of 1.8 per cent. Doesn't look quite so good now does it? Of course this calculation may not deter you, and that's fine, so long as you base your investment decision on the real, net, return and don't fall into the trap of just seeing the headline figure.

> **THIS IS ABOUT DECIDING IF AND WHEN YOU'RE GOING TO GET THAT HOUSE OR THAT HOLIDAY**

Here's another example. Suppose you buy a property to rent out. If it costs you, say, £200,000 and you let it out at £10,000 a year, you might think that looks pretty good. But hang on – what have you got to factor in before you make your decision? Well, there's the cost of the mortgage of course. And the insurance. The letting agent's fees. Maybe periods when the property is empty between tenants. Oh, and tax on the rental income. See? I'm not saying buy-to-let is never worth it, but you've got to calculate the net return before you can decide if this is a good move for you. Obviously there's also the potential capital growth in a property to consider, but that's not guaranteed except perhaps over the very long term. Certainly if you need to sell the property in five or even ten years' time, you can't assume significant growth, and the value may even have dropped.

So do your sums. They're not complicated, but they do require you to think it through and make sure you haven't forgotten anything – especially the tax you may eventually have to pay on anything you make.

If you see money as the solution you'll find it becomes the problem

Having money doesn't make all your relationships flow smoothly – not by a long shot. It doesn't protect you from disease – it may buy you better medical care after the event but it doesn't protect you. It might buy a better diet but the rich half of the world has a pretty poor health record despite having all the money to feed itself extremely well, so wealth and health do not necessarily go hand in hand.

> **IT MAY BUY YOU BETTER MEDICAL CARE AFTER THE EVENT BUT IT DOESN'T PROTECT YOU**

The more you see money as a solution, the greater the chance that you are missing the point entirely. Money doesn't do anything.

I know, I know. You'll be thinking, 'If only I had X amount, I could fix this problem in my life'. I think you'll find money would throw up a lot more problems in its wake. Money will not make you happier, thinner or more popular with decent people. Money does not deliver lasting, meaningful peace of mind. There are plenty of rich, fat, unhappy people with no real friends. I think we need to find the cure to our problems first and then find a way of funding that cure. Money isn't, and never will be, the cure. It is the oil that smoothes the wheels. It isn't the engine.

RULE 13

You can make lots of money, you can enjoy your job, and you can sleep nights

A lot of people hold one or other – or all – of these notions:

- Making money goes hand in hand with being a ruthless, manipulative, amoral, greedy lizard.

- To make a bit of cash you have to sell your soul, grandmother and principles.

- Being wealthy means you end up with a heart problem, insomnia and other stress-related disorders.

- To make money you have to turn into a slimeball who sacrifices their family, morals and happiness and all on the altar of wealth.

Well, it can be like that, but it doesn't have to be. In fact, it shouldn't be. That's the beauty of it. If it *is* like that, then you're doing it wrong. You see, money is so freely available – and to anyone (as we looked at in Rule 1) – that you really don't need to try that hard, or change that much. An awful lot of pretty ordinary, nice people make money – and lots of it.

You *can* make money, enjoy your job and sleep at night. You just have to decide that is what you're going to do – no matter what. And then stick to it.

Remember, if you are starting to lose sleep or have stopped enjoying what you do, then you need to have a serious talk with yourself. Go back to the beginning of the book and remember what it is that wealth is all about to you.

I remember a cartoon of a boardroom with fat-cat executives. A small girl pokes her head round the door and says, 'Money can't buy a kind smile'. The businessmen all look, momentarily, shamed. Then the chairman growls, 'Get outta here, kid, who the hell wants a kind smile?' and the others all look relieved and go back to their meeting.

Well, I for one would like the kind smile even if it does mean I lose a little money. I want to sleep nights and to enjoy my job and to make money. But I won't compromise my principles, spend too little time with my family or children, neglect to sit in the sunshine occasionally, take a day off. I won't worry about work or money once I've gone to bed, be driven so much by money that I lose my sense of humour or need to have fun. These I swear by. And it is possible – believe me, I've known and observed enough wealthy people to know this is true – to make money and have a life, to be ethical and rich, to earn a lot and be a thoroughly nice person. It is possible. It just sometimes seems it isn't. All part of debunking our money myths.

> **IF YOU LOSE SLEEP OR HAVE STOPPED ENJOYING WHAT YOU DO, THEN YOU NEED TO HAVE A TALK WITH YOURSELF**

RULE 14

Don't make money by being bad

I like Google's corporate motto – 'Don't be evil'. It's probably an anagram of something but I still like it. If you have to lie, cheat, steal, defraud, lose sleep, hide, dodge the law in any way, break the rules or generally behave badly to make your money, then don't do it, it isn't worth it.

If earning money or being wealthy stops being fun – and by being bad it really will stop being fun – then there's no point doing it. If you don't enjoy the challenge of earning money in a decent way, then best go and do something different.

I knew a major criminal once. He told me it was no fun being 'bent' as, in fact, he had to be a lot more law-abiding than the rest of us. He couldn't risk getting pulled over by the police for speeding or any minor motoring offence; no late night parties in case the police got called out; no flash car to draw attention to himself; no lavish lifestyle in case it put him in the spotlight.

> **IF YOU DON'T ENJOY THE CHALLENGE OF EARNING MONEY IN A DECENT WAY THEN GO AND DO SOMETHING DIFFERENT**

But there is more to living a clean life than being able to speed or have parties. Living a life where you make your money from being good lets you sleep nights. You get to look your kids in the eye – and yourself in the mirror – with the added bonus of a feel-good factor. No amount of money can buy that.

If you have to resort to being wicked, it means you've failed; you've lost the plot. It means you haven't been able to do it properly. It means you're scraping the barrel. It means you haven't been able to think of a proper idea. It means you've been lazy, desperate, non-creative, boring.

I can come up with lots of examples of famous wealthy people who've made their money out of being bad. Yep, they're wealthy it's true, but look in their eyes and what do you see there? Do you want to have that stay-awake-at-night-worrying look? Do you want that flinch-when-the-doorbell-rings kind of life? You want nobody-trusts-you sort of relationships? Or would you rather relax and know that you did it legit, honest, fairly? It's a no-brainer really, isn't it?

As long as you can earn your wealth without ripping people off, being cruel or unjust, breaking the law or bending the rules, you'll be doing fine. All it requires is a quick check, staying conscious of what you – and your money – are doing.

Money and happiness – understand their relationship

There are lots of things that will make us miserable – losing a partner, being made redundant, getting sick. And loads more. There are quite a few related to money and gaining or spending thereof.

Remember:

- too little money can make you miserable
- too much money can make you miserable
- too much stuff can make you miserable
- not having enough stuff can make you miserable.

I think what we have to grasp pretty well from Day 1 is that money and happiness are not necessarily the same thing. *Money doesn't buy happiness.* This is a common mistake people make. It isn't going to be one you make. You can be poor and happy. You can be rich and happy. You can also be either poor or rich and miserable.

If you are looking to wealth to make you happy, you'll be disappointed. If you are looking to money to make you powerful/younger/sexier/more vital/more interesting/better looking/whatever, you're going to be disappointed. Sorry but money doesn't do any of that. In your head it might. In other people's heads it might. But it doesn't in reality. You can be all those things with money, it is true. It isn't money that does it. The switch is thrown in your head first. Money is a placebo, not a cure.

We've all seen the lottery winners who buy the big house and feel miserable because they've left all their friends behind. Or the tycoons who lose the lot and top themselves because they felt their life was over just because they were skint.

> # MONEY IS A PLACEBO,
> # NOT A CURE

But we won't make any of these mistakes because we shall practise this Rule diligently and understand the relationship between money and happiness. Ah, but I hear you ask, what exactly is this Rule? What do I have to do? Answer: nothing except not expect too much from money and don't buy stuff in the hope it will make you happy – it won't. When they build that brand new Beemer or whatever it is you covet, they don't build in any happiness. So when you first sit in it or buy it and you feel fantastic – and I'm not denying people do feel great buying stuff – that feeling isn't in the thing you buy. That feeling was inside you anyway. All this said, what money can do is buy away a lot of *un*happiness. It just can't go any further than that.

RULE 16

Know the difference between price and value

I once asked my delightful father-in-law to explain that thing about wine to me. You know, can a bottle that costs £100 in a top restaurant *really* be 20 times as good as a bottle that you can get for a fiver at the local shop?

His answer was interesting. He said that you aren't paying for the wine alone. What you are paying for is the ambience, the service, the location (we're talking Le Gavroche here), the wine waiter's expertise, the good company, the fine tablecloths, the privacy and discretion, the style and class, the tradition, the food and the trust, the humidity and storage, the tone and the surroundings, the fellow dining guests and the great conversation.

The wine is almost an irrelevance and that's the point. We think we know the price of something. But the value can spread out far beyond all of that.

I have an old Mercedes car (I like Mercs but am far too mean to buy a new one and lose all that depreciation). I didn't pay much for it. You never do, as people are scared of them in case they go wrong, and fair enough they do cost a fortune to put right, *but* you need to remember that because they are better made, they rarely do go wrong. I was visited by a friend who was driving a brand new car he'd just bought. A modern Eurobox, a small hatchback thing that looked like a mini spaceship. He looked at my old, battered, mud-streaked Merc and exclaimed, 'Blimey, you must be doing well!' I tried to explain that wasn't the case and that he'd probably paid at least five times for his what I'd paid for mine but he wouldn't have it. He saw the Merc and had decided its value was a lot more than the price – i.e. what was actually paid for it. I learnt that day about price not necessarily equating to perceived value.

Remember too that something is only worth what others are willing to pay for it. A catalogue may say the value of a painting is £500 but that's only true if somebody is willing to pay that amount for it. An important lesson to learn. The price of something can be far less than its actual value, either to you or to somebody else. Or a lot more.

If you are going to be wealthy – and I sincerely hope you are, if you put into play the Rules in this book and work diligently at it – then it's worth studying the difference between price and value.

> WE THINK WE KNOW THE
> PRICE OF SOMETHING. BUT
> THE VALUE CAN SPREAD OUT
> FAR BEYOND ALL OF THAT

RULE 17

Know how the wealthy think

There is a simple test to determine whether someone will end up wealthy – or if they already are. All you have to do is watch someone read their favourite newspaper, especially if it's one of the big Sundays:

- Notice which paper they choose.

- Notice which sections they choose to read.

- Notice which sections they discard.

- Notice in which order they read their chosen sections.

This is a test for you too. Have a look at the above and make a mental note of what *you* do. The wealthy – those who have deliberately chosen to be wealthy rather than those who have won the lottery or inherited (God's lottery as I think of it) or married into it – invariably:

- choose the more serious papers

- choose the more serious sections

- discard the 'frivolous' sections

- read the money/business sections first.

If you are serious about being wealthy, you will have to learn how the wealthy think. This means studying the 'opposition' – although very shortly you will be a part of them. You need to know the lingo and the language, where they eat and live, how they work and relax, how they invest and save. In short, you need to study money if you are to increase your prosperity. Try to get to talk to wealthy people. Ask questions. Develop a thirst for understanding and knowledge. Read about wealthy people – interviews and autobiographies can be full of insight.

YOU NEED TO STUDY MONEY IF YOU ARE TO INCREASE YOUR PROSPERITY

You may also benefit from a few well-chosen business and finance books. I'm not going to recommend any to you as I don't know your reading style – find ones that suit you. Also, why not log on to the FT site or the finance pages of other online papers to keep up with the latest developments in the money market? Get informed.

But what if this all feels a bit too heavy? If, like me, you like the gossip columns as well as financial pages then you, like me, will probably never be extremely, mind-bogglingly over-the-top wealthy. We can still be wealthy – and we might have more fun too. Prosperous and fun – sounds good to me. I think we have to be really passionate about money if we want lots. We have to live and breathe and sleep (yes, bearing in mind Rule 13) money. We have to study hard at the University of Wealth if we want to graduate.

Don't envy what others have

We all set our own objectives. We all have individual ambitions. We all work out how much work we are prepared to put into this business of becoming wealthy. We all set our own limits and know what we are prepared to do or not do. So what is the point of envying what anyone else has? None, unless you know what their agenda was and is. None, unless you know how much work they were prepared to put in. None, unless you know what they were prepared to sacrifice.

Of course you can cast an envious glance at the easy three – lottery, inherited, married (or divorced!) into – we all do. But money earned is entirely the business of the person earning it. They did the work. They had the idea or entrepreneurial spirit. They got up earlier than us. They were driven or fired up by what they wanted to achieve. Envying them is pointless; learning from them is invaluable.

And learning from them is the greatest gift they can give us. Ideally you need a money mentor. Someone you look up to who has made a lot of money and in the right way – legally, enjoyably and nicely – who will give you the odd tip, tuck you under their wing, set you on the right path. And refuse to lend you any money of course. Not that you'd ask.

If I come across someone extremely rich, I immediately try to work out how they did it and if that route would suit me. What bits of information could I glean to help me get to that position, bearing in mind I only want to do it right – legally and enjoyably?

I think 90 per cent of getting these Rules right is to approach getting wealthy as sympathetic magic – do as they do and you'll end up as them.

I have my money mentor and I hang on to his every word when it comes to money as he's living on the interest on the interest on his money – and that's the place I'm heading for.

Use other people as a source of inspiration. Besides, envy is not a characteristic of a Rules Player – that's you now, by the way.

ENVYING THEM IS POINTLESS;

LEARNING FROM THEM IS

INVALUABLE

It's harder to manage yourself than it is to manage your money

So how well do you know yourself? Pretty well? Not at all? Vaguely? We think we know ourselves until we come to give up smoking, lose weight, get fit, get rich. And then we realize we are lazier, have less willpower, less determination, make less effort, get too easily dissuaded, fall by the wayside too readily.

If I wanted to tuck you under my wing and make you wealthy, the first thing I would need to know is: 'Do you have what it takes to be wealthy? Are you determined enough? Will you work hard enough? Will you stick at it? Do you have backbone? Stamina? Guts? Relentless focus?' You see, if you don't, the chances are you won't succeed. I'm not trying to put you off. I am trying to make you see that making money is a skill that can be taught – as long as the person is ready and willing to learn and apply themselves diligently.

> ## THE FIRST THING I WOULD NEED TO KNOW IS: 'DO YOU HAVE WHAT IT TAKES TO BE WEALTHY?'

If you decided you wanted to win Wimbledon you would have needed to start playing tennis when you were about five and have been winning junior championships by the time you were fourteen. It's the same with money. You can't expect an overweight, middle-aged person to suddenly be in the final.

When I was a young struggling student I once sold a valuable book so I could eat. I made a direct choice between owning something that was going to increase in value, and thus potentially make me wealthy, and having a slap-up meal for one. You see what I mean? I, in essence, chose – at that time anyway – to be poor rather than wealthy. I saw the same book recently in a bookshop and, believe me, I made a bad call that day.

And what I have noticed is that the wealthy – when they are starting out anyway – have enormous drive and are prepared to make enormous sacrifices. They manage themselves and forgo instant rewards for bigger payback in the longer term. Self-control and delayed gratification are useful arts to learn.

GETTING
WEALTHY

We've entered the dark uncharted waters of Part Two. This is where we get serious. This is where we start the real practical stuff. This is where you have to start taking a good hard look at your situation, doing some planning and taking some action.

Getting wealthy means being very honest with yourself and being willing to invest your time and efforts into the quest for greater prosperity. Many of the Rules are behavioural and changing your behaviour is never easy. Some Rules will seem stunningly simple, but for every Rule you have to ask yourself: 'I may already know this – but do I do it?' The willingness to put in the graft and do something, make things happen, is vital.

RULE 20

You've got to know where you are before you start

Before we can go forward we have to know where we are now. Or rather *you* have to. When Robinson Crusoe swam ashore from his shipwrecked boat, the first thing he did was check out what stores and guns and ammunition he had. Once he knew that, he could assess the situation and move forward.

> ## WE HAVE TO KNOW
> ## WHERE WE ARE NOW

So you are going to swim ashore and begin your new life. The first thing you have to do is to take stock. Find out what you've already got, what can be used, what can be discarded or discounted, what you owe, what you are owed, what basically is your net worth.

We're going to do a full financial audit on you and your life. If you don't know where you are before you start, you can't really work efficiently towards becoming wealthy. It's a wise man who lays out his tools before he begins the job.

Here's your check list. It may need adapting to suit your individual circumstances. Start with the big figures to get a picture of where you are right now overall:

Item	+	−
House/mortgage		
Credit/store cards		
Bank		
Savings		
Pension		
Loans/overdraft		
Assets/cars etc.		
Personal items – jewellery etc.		
Investments		
Debts		
TOTAL NET WORTH		

Now you have an overall figure, you need to look at your typical inflow and outflow of cash on a monthly or annual basis – you can choose which you assess, but all figures have to be made either monthly or annual.

Put your income here:		
Item	−	Balance
Fixed regular expenditure (e.g. insurance, bills, food, memberships)		
Variable regular expenditure (e.g. shopping, holidays)		
TOTALS		

This may not be ideal for your circumstances but I'm sure you get the idea. Don't be tempted to skip this exercise. Even if your financial situation is none too rosy, it's good to face up to reality so you can take positive action to address the situation.

You've got to have a plan

Why are a fool and his money so easily parted? Because the fool doesn't have a plan. If you don't have a plan you'll be tempted to fritter your cash away, spend it instead of investing, or forget the new business idea or career move. If you have a plan you know exactly what does and what doesn't fit into it.

The last Rule helped you work out where you are now, and you already know where you're going (your objective). The plan gives you the important bit – how you are going to get there. Back to the Robinson Crusoe analogy. Once he had been shipwrecked and taken stock he made a plan. 'I'll need a shelter to keep warm, some food, and something to do.' And he set about building a thatched shelter on the beach, which of course got blown over in the first gale and he had to retreat inland to a cave. You see, even the best plans have to be open to adjustment.

> **THE PLAN GIVES YOU THE IMPORTANT BIT – HOW YOU ARE GOING TO GET THERE**

First things first. If you have a job you love and are happy then you'll probably want to stick at it. If it doesn't make you enough money, you need a plan to generate income another way. If your job is making you miserable and what's worse keeping you in a poverty trap then you must prioritize getting out of it in your plan.

Your plan should involve taking financial control of your life. If you have debts, it will definitely include tackling these as a priority, ditto spending excesses. The plan might involve a career change, investigating a business idea, investing money or generating some capital so you can enter the buy-to-let market. It may well include selling things. A lot of money is generated through selling things – whether it's a product, a service or your time and skill. That's why I like writing books – even while I sleep there is a bookshop somewhere that is selling books for me. In fact one of the fundamental truths about gettng rich is that wealth – real wealth – comes from doing deals, not from earning wages, salaries or fees.

As General Patton said, 'A good plan today is better than a perfect plan tomorrow'. Whatever the plan includes, just make sure you have one, and that you stick to it. Don't worry, the rest of this book will give you lots of ideas as to what your plan could contain. Just remember: never sit back and wait for somebody to give you money – ever.

RULE 22

Get your finances under control

There's been a huge fuss made over the last few years in the UK about hosepipe bans. If you live elsewhere this may be a complete mystery. It's even a mystery to me to be honest. In the UK there are companies that are allowed to collect water in reservoirs and then sell it to householders. The reservoirs have been low recently due to a lack of rain – apparently. If you live in the UK you'll know that it never stops raining. A lot of the householders are saying that there is a shortage of water because the water utility companies don't repair their pipes and masses of water leaks away. The poor householders are being told they can't water their gardens because there isn't enough water. They say there is enough water and that they are being punished unfairly. See where I'm going with this?

You may well have enough money but it leaks away before you get to spend it. In a whole variety of ways – taxation, paying interest, lack of use (not invested properly), too much being spent on the wrong things. Before you can control your finances you have to stop the leaks.

If you carried out the exercise in Rule 20 (of course you did) you'll have a record of your credit card balances. Higher than you cared to admit? Probably. We are all encouraged to spend on plastic. We are all seduced into racking up debts monthly. If you want to stop the leaks, cut up all the cards and pay them off.*

---

* 'And spend what?' I hear you ask. Spend what you can afford on what you have to, and above that spend nothing for a while. Make the choice: wealth or spending sprees. You've tried the spending sprees. We all have. Now take the prosperity route and see if it isn't better. You are only postponing spending, not cancelling it forever. You'll also be able to spend more later. Look forward to that as you tighten your belt. Think of the better belt you'll be able to buy.

BEFORE YOU CAN CONTROL YOUR FINANCES YOU HAVE TO STOP THE LEAKS

Do a quick calculation and see what levels of interest you are paying. It's the same with your mortgage. Make sure you're not paying more than you have to through negligence. If your fixed rate deal has come to an end it could be time to check out the best deals that are now available.

Keep a record of everything you spend. *Everything.* Do this for a short while – even just a week – and see where the leakages are. If you are going to be wealthy, first you have to know where your money is going. Sorry if you thought this was going to be easy or this book was going to be full of get-rich-quick schemes. But stick with me, and you'll be glad you did.

When you carry out your financial stock-check, watch out for the hidden things which can easily be overlooked. For instance, direct debits and subscriptions that are too high, wrong or out of date. The rich are eagle-eyed and miss nothing.

Insurance pays someone, and odds are it's not you

Just think this one through with me. Insurance companies set their premiums so that on balance (if not on every contract) they'll make money. At whose expense? Yours of course. Suppose you pay £100 a year over 10 years, that'll be £1000 in total. The insurer will have calculated that the odds are they'll pay out less than £1000 in total for whatever-it-is you're insuring. In which case it would have cost you less to pay the costs of repairs/replacement/medical care or whatever, than it was to pay your insurance premiums.

It doesn't matter what you're insuring, or who with. This is just the way that insurance companies make their money. Plus they have admin costs, overheads, marketing costs and all the rest to cover, and they'll have factored those into your premiums too. In fact, most people don't get back more than two-thirds of the money they pay in insurance, even long term. So it just doesn't make financial sense to take out insurance on all your pets, property, washing machines and so on.

Having said that, there are two instances where you are better off taking out insurance. The first is, of course, where it's a legal necessity, such as driver's insurance. You just have to swallow that one.

The other instance is if you don't have enough in your bank to pay out the lump sum if the worst happens. Say you don't insure your pet, and then they need an operation costing £1000 – will you be able to find the money all at once? If not, what would you do? Maybe you'll feel you'd rather pay out more over the years in insurance for the peace of mind it gives you. Then, if Tibbles gets a fishbone stuck in his throat when you're having a particularly tight month financially, you can still afford the op.

There are a few tricky ones, such as health insurance, but where you're insuring property, pets or white goods it's pretty straightforward. It doesn't matter what goes wrong with your washing machine, you know the most it can set you back is the cost of a new machine. Could you afford that? If so, you're wasting your money on insurance.

Have you added up how much you're spending every month on insurance premiums? Well, why not? Go and do it now. Now think about what you could do with that money if you weren't paying for all that insurance. If you just put it in a savings account it would at least earn a little interest.

And that's something that the canniest wealth-builders do. If they're worried about losing the cash flow safety-net of insurance, they cancel their contracts and then ringfence that amount each month in a savings account. If they have a sudden problem with Tibbles or their washing machine or anything else, the money is there for just such emergencies. Meanwhile it still belongs to them, along with the interest, rather than to the insurance company. And that extra third most of us pay out and never get back – well, that's still theirs too, to spend or save as they wish.

> MOST PEOPLE DON'T GET BACK MORE THAN TWO-THIRDS OF THE MONEY THEY PAY IN INSURANCE, EVEN LONG TERM

Only by looking wealthy can you become wealthy

I once watched a man looking at a job vacancy board. He was dressed in scruffy trainers, wore a hood (up), was unshaven and slouched with his hands in his pockets. You just knew he was going to go for job interviews dressed like that – and fail to get them. And then he'd claim it was unfair, nobody would give him a break, life sucks and so on.

I've held many job interviews and have always been seriously under-impressed with the way people turned up. The lack of effort is always staggering – as is the lack of research and interest. 'Why do you want to work for this company?' 'Dunno.' 'What do we do here?' 'Dunno.'

I'm trying not to be an old reactionary here. But I can't fail to notice that the lack of effort is directly related to the lack of results. The poor look poor. Not because they have to. They wear a uniform that marks them out. If they change that uniform they change their circumstances because people will react differently to them. We aren't too far removed from the great apes and they relate to each other based a lot on how they move and look. Those who look weak and needy are treated as such. The powerful will strut and look confident. What I am suggesting is that you need to look powerful and confident. We should all look powerful and confident.

Ah, but how can we afford to dress as if we are more wealthy? Come on, come on. I expected better of you. Think laterally. The great apes do it with no clothes at all. It's about the way you walk rather than what you wear. It's about the overall image you project.

But this doesn't mean you can get away with dressing inappropriately or badly – anyone can dress smartly. Borrow a decent outfit or buy a good suit cheaply (no, no, don't buy full price and just put it on your credit card). For the interview for my first casino job, I bought a fabulous jacket from a charity shop – double breasted, wide satin lapels – and proper bow tie you had to tie yourself (none of those rubbish ones on elastic for me). I practised for hours until I got it right and turned up for the first night looking more James Bond than trainee. I made a dramatic impression. Obviously I had got it wrong and had to go and buy a simple black suit from the high street afterwards, but I was remembered as somehow standing out, stylish not scruffy. And I got offered the plum trainee job despite not being in any way qualified for it.

This stuff works you know. Dress wealthy and people will assume you are and treat you accordingly. Learn style, class, how the wealthy dress. Look poor and you'll get poor service. And whatever you do, no bling. Yes, rich rap stars can get away with it but you can't. Nor can I. Restrained elegance is what we shall aim for. Old money. Quality. Simple lines. Good haircut. Clean nails. You know the sort of stuff I mean.

RULE 25

Speculate to accumulate (no, this isn't gambling)

We all know the actor who achieves overnight fame after one starring role and everyone says how lucky they must have been. Luck? They starred in every school production. Studied at drama school for three years. Worked their socks off in some dreadful soap. Slaved on the stage for the whole run of *Mind Your Manners* by Agatha Christie. Played an extra in *Extras*. Did panto every Christmas – playing the pumpkin of course. And finally landed their plum job, their starring role, in some deservedly successful film. And everyone says, 'How lucky you are!'

Getting wealthy is a bit like that. You toil away for years and suddenly you are lucky. You scrimp and save and sacrifice and gosh, how wonderful to be touched by fate's fickle finger!

> ## YOU TOIL AWAY FOR YEARS
> ## AND SUDDENLY YOU
> ## ARE LUCKY

Well, the truth is that you have to speculate to accumulate. You have to be in it to win it. If you don't bet, you don't get. No, no, no. I am not suggesting gambling in any sense. If you invest on the Stock Exchange, after wisely taking advice and studying the companies and their performance, this is the safest form of gambling. If you stake it all on red, this is high-risk gambling.

If you work your socks off for 20 years and finally it pays off, this is not gambling.

Speculate has in fact four meanings – to discuss, to think deeply, to invest and to believe in something not entirely certain. I think that about sums up our pathway to prosperity.

- **Discuss**. Talk to all and sundry about wealth and see what others think and do. Study them closely.

- **Think deeply**. Understand your subject.

- **Invest**. Speculate with your time and effort and life.

- **Believe in something not entirely certain**. There are no guarantees, but you should be able to shorten the odds considerably if you follow the rules others have forged for you.

I know you might have thought I mean you to speculate with your hard-earned cash. I don't. I mean you to speculate with your time and effort, forethought and planning, energy and dedication. The more you put in, the more you'll get out.

On the other hand you could go and blow it all on red. Only joking.

RULE 26

Decide your attitude to risk

Am I going to suggest that money can only be hard won by perilous investments and chancy ventures? No, I'm not. In that case, am I suggesting caution and that you should carefully hang on to every penny? No, I'm not advocating that either.

What I am suggesting is that it's entirely up to you what level of risk you feel happy with – it's no good me telling you what that level should be. You have to decide your own attitude to and appetite for risk. Personally I love the *idea* of sailing close to the wind financially. However, my attitude is definitely verging on the cautious side so I don't take the risk. I find the risky schemes where you could blow the lot or make a fortune hold some appeal but I don't indulge my whims. I have young children and they come first.

Once you have decided your attitude to risk it makes your planning easier. It allows you to tailor how you intend becoming prosperous. Hare or tortoise I guess.

> IT'S ENTIRELY UP TO YOU
> WHAT LEVEL OF RISK YOU
> FEEL HAPPY WITH

Obviously your attitude will vary depending on the project. Things to take into consideration are:

- **Your age**. We cope better with risk the younger we are.

- **Family commitments**. If, like me, you have young children it does make you more cautious. If they've all left home, you might be prepared to push it a bit further.

- **Income and/or assets**. You need to work out the percentage of your wealth you are prepared to risk. The more you've got, the smaller the risk might be – unless you are prepared to risk the lot of course.

If you are going to take risks, then do try to offset them. Take out insurance if you like. Also:

- Don't put all your eggs in one basket (more about this later).

- Consider how much stress and excitement you can handle.

- Look at the timing – long term against quick returns.

- Think about how much you can afford to risk. Worst-case scenario stuff.

- Judge how much information you have. Too little increases risk.

The other thing to ponder is how you respond to the risks of life. Life in itself is risky and nothing is certain. How do you cope when things go wrong? Are you positive, dynamic, enthusiastic and up? Or do you get all gloomy and depressed and feel the glass is half empty? Know yourself and know how you cope and how you respond to changes. And remember that risk doesn't mean bad. It means you don't know how it will all turn out.

Think through the alternatives to taking a risk

We all know that the greater the risk, the higher the potential reward. And of course the lower the risk, the less return you're likely to get on your investment.

But you also need to consider what your alternative is. What if you don't take this risk? Is there an alternative that gives you almost as high a return, or will the money bring you in almost nothing if you don't take the risk?

Let me give you an example. Suppose you're considering investing in a volatile market for a chance of high returns. If you don't make the investment, you could put the money in the building society where it ought to be safe (I did say *ought* to...). So what kind of interest is the building society paying you? It could be 3 per cent. Then again, it could be 0.5 per cent. If it's fairly high, your high risk investment may not be worth taking, whereas when interest rates are very low it might be your best chance of a decent return.

This concept – the overall reward you get for taking a risk, when measured against the alternatives, is called risk premium (just forget that bit if you don't like jargon, I only put it there in case you want to know). It's a calculation particularly worth making when it comes to short-term investments, as over the long term it can be harder to predict how the alternatives to the risk will perform.

Look back to late 2007. Then, savers could get interest rates of over 6 per cent. At the same time, the equity markets (share prices) were falling. So there was no reward, or premium, for taking the risk of investing in equities. However, once interest rates dropped the balance shifted and equities looked like a far better option than they had – and that has nothing to do with the investments themselves, but simply how they measured up against the alternatives.

> ## YOU NEED TO CONSIDER WHAT YOUR ALTERNATIVE IS. WHAT IF YOU DON'T TAKE THIS RISK?

If you don't trust someone, don't do business with them

It's such a simple rule: we don't do business with people we don't trust. What more is there to say? Apart from that this also includes companies, corporations, governments, you name it. And why don't we trust them? Because there is something adrift, something that rings that little warning bell inside us. There may be clear visible signs but as often as not there won't be. Mostly this rule is about using your intuition, listening to your inner voice.

If you feel something, anything, is wrong, then walk away. Listen to what is being said to you. There are unconscious clues your subconscious is picking up. If you ignore them you'll invariably regret it. I've done it. We've all done it. I nearly did it again the other day. I nearly bought a car from a dodgy dealer. I knew he was dodgy but I wanted the car. I knew the car would be dodgy. What is it that makes us overwrite all the warning signs? I did the only sensible thing – I phoned a friend. And he talked me out of it. Good man.

You can extend this rule to cover loads of situations such as: 'If you don't trust your boss, don't work for them.' 'If you don't trust your childminder, don't leave your kids with them.' 'If you don't feel comfortable with your financial adviser, get another.'

Look, you can choose what you do and how you do it but if you want to be a Rules Player then you need to be assertive, stand up for what you know is right, don't accept second best – ever. Listen to your intuition, be the biggest, boldest and bravest. If the situation feels wrong, it probably is. If you don't get the right feelings about a person you are dealing with, find a way out.

If it waddles like a duck and quacks like a duck, chances are it's a duck. Avoid. Walk away. Hold on to your wallet and run.

> ## LISTEN TO YOUR INTUITION, BE THE BIGGEST, BOLDEST AND BRAVEST

It's never too late to start getting wealthy

It's very easy sometimes to believe that the hand we got dealt in life is all we have to play with. Or to say, 'Ah well, I should have started a pension in my early twenties – it's too late now'. But we can change anything we want – it's never too late to start being wealthy.

Look at Rule 1 again – anyone can make money. And it's not limited by your age or any other time factor. All it requires is that you shift your focus to becoming wealthy and already things will happen without you having to do anything more. Obviously if you want more than the basic that the universe is going to give you, you will have to do more. But by shifting your focus you will set wheels in motion and prosperity will come to you. And no, this isn't mumbo jumbo. It's a universal fact. The fact you do something – shift your focus – is enough.

No matter how long you have been going along a particular path – poverty, lack of success, whatever – it doesn't need much of a shift to alter course. And altering course can happen no matter how long you've left it. There is no such thing as too late. It's a bit like being an ocean-going liner. You may need a lot of space to stop but it doesn't take much to get you to change direction. A couple of degrees on the wheel and you'll be on a completely different course within a few miles.

In gaining prosperity, as in most things, there is a tipping point. Once you've added on those couple of degrees to port or starboard the resulting change in trajectory gets bigger and bigger in a sort of compound way.

It is also never too late to start investing – in stocks, in shares, in a pension, in style, in quality, in yourself, in life. By staying alert and alive we resist that decline into inactivity and apathy which is such an ageing attitude. My father-in-law (always such an inspiration) started another business when he was 75, and not just any old business either – it was in a new technology which most 50-year-olds were having trouble getting their head round.

> # IT IS NEVER TOO LATE TO START INVESTING – IN SHARES, IN A PENSION, IN STYLE, IN QUALITY, IN YOURSELF, IN LIFE

However, if you think it is too late, it probably is. The secret is never to think that. If you think that you can give up easily then you probably will. Don't think it. Look, we came into this book together to make money – some for you and some for me. I'm going to do my bit, my damnedest, to help you increase your prosperity. If you think there are any barriers – age, sex, race, ability – then you are already batting on a losing wicket. Dump the preconceptions and trust me. It is never too late to begin. Start now.

RULE 30

Start saving young (or teach your kids this one if it's too late for you)

OK, it might be too late for you to start saving young. We can't go back. But you can certainly teach your kids the importance of learning this trick. And I'm not suggesting we scrimp and save to be able to save. Saving should be something we naturally do. I guess it's a trick you learn quickly if you are self-employed – or not, if you go bust. Every time you earn money you put some aside for VAT and tax. Failure to do so means scrabbling around when the return is due and you have to find it. If you put aside more than you need, the leftovers become the savings. Obviously you only fail to do this once or twice before it becomes a really easy thing to remember to do.

> ## IF YOU PUT ASIDE
> ## MORE THAN YOU NEED,
> ## THE LEFTOVERS BECOME
> ## THE SAVINGS

I find that it is easier to have a 'figure' so you don't have to think too much. My own figure is 50 per cent. Anything I earn, I put half straight into a savings account. I don't have to think about this. I know that some is for tax and some is for VAT and the rest is for savings. Every now and again I transfer the balance of what's left to a second savings account – a sort of super savings account. From the super savings account I can transfer money to a pension fund, ISA (Individual Savings Account) or whatever.

This, for me, is an easy way to save. I don't have to think too much about it. It is a method I pass on to my children – spend half your pocket money and save half. I hope they'll find this an easy method to pick up, a sort of savings muscle memory, so that they will have a quid or two when they need it at university or whatever.

I really wish I had (a) started saving young and (b) been taught to do so. Lots of really prosperous people have said that they had wealth management drummed into them from a very early age. It seems to be an essential part of prosperity gaining.

I am fascinated to watch my own children learning about money. There does seem to be a genetic predisposition for spending or saving. We treat all of them identically when it comes to money but one child finds it easy to save; another is a fanatic spender and couldn't save anything to save himself; and one is oblivious to money either way.

I'm a great believer in making changes to correct basic flaws in one's upbringing. It's no good sitting around blaming others, you have to change it. I have to take responsibility and train myself. Obviously this doesn't apply to being tidy.

Understand that your financial needs change at different stages of your life

Some cultures allow for a different focus, a different strategy, during different stages of your life. For instance, up to 20 might be for being young and foolish and getting an education. Age 20 to 35 could be for getting married and raising a family. Age 35 to 55 might be for running your business and making your fortune. Life after that is for spiritual contemplation and retirement from the commercial world.

> **ALLOW FOR A DIFFERENT FOCUS, A DIFFERENT STRATEGY, DURING DIFFERENT STAGES OF YOUR LIFE**

Essentially, your financial needs change over time, reflecting what is going on in your life at any stage, and the choices you make in your lifestyle at that time. You might need more money when raising a family, but maybe this is a time when you can usually cope better with a little adversity.

By the time your kids are at university you definitely need loads more cash or the poor darlings won't have enough to squander in the student union bar in the evenings, every evening. And once you hit retirement you can downsize again – unless you intend spending it all on expensive world cruises.

This rule is about checking where you are and what you need. And about knowing that the conditions which influence your needs do and will change. You have to make allowances for differing circumstances.

A bit of forward planning with this in mind will stand you in good stead. For example, if you're about to invest all your spare cash in a long-term investment scheme, remember that if you suddenly need a bit more money as you've taken maternity leave or you want to go on a world trip in a career break, your money will be tied up. Think it through and anticipate possible future needs and changes.

So, quick exercise. Where are you in your life? How much do you need? What is the next stage for you? How much are you going to need?

RULE 32

You have to work hard to get rich enough not to have to work hard

I cannot emphasize how strongly I feel about this one. I watch and learn from the seriously wealthy and have reached the conclusion that in nearly every single case they slogged their guts out to get where they are. They often started early. They worked late into the night. They sacrificed a lot. They didn't take long lunch breaks, they didn't waste time. They didn't watch television in the evenings. They worked their socks off. They know money doesn't grow on trees.

If you too are serious about getting rich, then you too must do as they do. You are going to have to put in the hard work to get rich enough so that you don't have to work hard. But you must do the work first.

So how dedicated are you? How serious are you? This is the point where we sort the wheat from the chaff, the men from the boys, the girls from the women, the runners-up from the winners.

Still here? Good. You are obviously committed. If you are prepared to put in the long hours and you put them in on the right things, you should succeed. Maybe not immediately. Maybe not with your first idea. But by slogging away you will get there. How do I know this? Because I have done it. I'm not preaching from the wilderness (I hope I'm not preaching at all). I started out poor, and worked long and hard and chose where to put my efforts carefully. And now I'm rich. It really is that simple. On the surface it looks like luck. But that's because I make it look so. In *The Rules of Work* I wrote about looking cool, looking laid back, looking effortless. I practise that a lot. I often go back to work very late at night after everyone else has gone to bed – or get up very early in the morning. Don't tell anyone because I like the indolent image where everyone assumes I am a work-shy, lotus-eating, decadent loafer. But the reality is I graft. You have to.

> # THEY DIDN'T WATCH TELEVISION IN THE EVENINGS. THEY WORKED THEIR SOCKS OFF

I'll let you into the secret of the wealthy club – you need to work like you've never worked before. Work like there is no one watching. Work like you don't have a boss. Work like your life depended on it. The second secret is that you have to enjoy it. If it's a chore then you won't do it.

Let me make one very important point here. This Rule does *not* mean that if you work hard at *anything* you will become wealthy. An office cleaner on the minimum wage will not become rich by working all hours as an office cleaner or by cleaning really hard and thoroughly. They might, however, become rich by starting their own cleaning company and working very hard at getting it off the ground, and finding new clients and making sure their staff were great, happy and motivated.

What I'm saying here is that even if you've got a great business idea or have some money to invest in shares, you will only maximize your return if you work really hard at your idea or invest the money wisely and manage it carefully. You have to put the effort in before you can reap the dividends.

Learn the art of deal making

Deals are great. Deals make you money. Simple deal-making skills will serve you time and time again. You need to learn to be bold, to ask for more, to trade what you have for what you want.

Here is an example of successful deal making in action. Kyle MacDonald from Montreal, Canada, traded his way from one single red paperclip to a house in the space of nine months. You can read more at http://oneredpaperclip.blogspot.com, but essentially this is how he did it:

- He launched his website offering to swap his one red paper clip for anything.
- He swapped it for a green pen in the shape of a fish.
- He swapped this for a smiley face doorknob.
- He swapped this for a portable barbeque.
- He swapped this for a portable generator.
- He swapped this for an instant party pack and keg of beer.
- He swapped this for a snowmobile.
- He swapped this for a trip to British Columbia.
- He swapped this for a truck.
- He swapped this for a recording contract.
- And finally he swapped this for a house in Phoenix, Colorado – admittedly only a year's lease but hey…

Eleven steps. Eleven little deals. Not bad. He says he is going to keep going until he owns a house. That's deal making.

So, lessons to be learnt from Kyle:

- Never say you haven't got anything to start with.

- Always be open to opportunities.

- Be adaptable and flexible.

- Have a goal.

- Work diligently.

- Network like mad.

- Take advantage of free publicity.

In my business I prefer to talk about 'mutually profitable partnerships'. These deals, where both parties benefit, are the best deals of all. Everybody feels happy with the outcome.

What do you have that others might want? Think broadly here – not just possessions like Kyle, but also your skills and your knowledge. Your time and your ability and efforts. Who might want these and what might you be able to ask for in return?

> # WHAT DO YOU HAVE THAT OTHERS MIGHT WANT?

Learn the art of negotiating

If you are going to deal and trade and swap, you have to learn the art of negotiating. Basically the art revolves around making the other person feel they are getting as much as you are.

I like to talk about partnerships. This is my way of making this happen. I'm genuinely not out to scupper anyone else's plans of getting rich. I don't need them to fail in order to make me succeed. I figure we can all go forward together and no one has to lose out. If I want someone to buy something from me I expect them to be able to make a profit on it and do well out of it. I don't want to sell and run. I want repeat business. I want a decent reputation. I want to feel good about what I do. I want a partnership.

The art of negotiating will stand you in good stead in so many different situations – from negotiating a simple pay rise to negotiating in your relationship with your partner to negotiating with your kids over pocket money. If you learn this art, everything slips along easily and smoothly and you get what you want – and they get what they want too. Win/win.

There are a number of rules about negotiating you need to bear in mind. Here are just a few of the most important ones:

- Always know your bottom line – the point beyond which you will not go.

- Always know what it is you want – the goal, the end product, the target. There's no use negotiating if you don't know what you are negotiating for.

- Always aim for win/win.

- Always be prepared to give up things to secure other things – be flexible and fluid.

- Always know as much as possible before you start – knowledge is power in these situations.

- Go for the best deal you can possibly justify. Coming down later is easy; going up later is almost impossible.

Those are just a few of the key points, but if you don't know this stuff backwards, buy a book, go on a course, talk to friends who really understand the skill of negotiating.

I am always stunned and horrified by how often people go into situations – anything from a job to a relationship – without first finding out what they are embarking on, what is expected of them, what they are going to get out of it, what they expect their partner (boss, business buddy, lover, offspring, whoever) to get out of it and where they expect to end up. You've got to discuss these things – and that really is the basic art, discussion. Bring things out into the open so there are no assumptions. Assumptions are bad.

> ## I DON'T WANT TO SELL AND RUN. I WANT REPEAT BUSINESS. I WANT A DECENT REPUTATION

Small economies won't make you wealthy but they will make you miserable

Is it penny wise, pound foolish? I don't think so. I think that trying to make small economies in order to become prosperous is doomed to failure. It won't make you rich but it will make you miserable. And being miserable isn't a good place to start out each day. You need a decent breakfast and a positive attitude. Cutting out your daily cappuccino might help you lose weight, and it might reduce your caffeine intake, but it isn't going to make you rich and it might well make you feel miserable.

So what about all that penny-pinching stuff? It seems to have been invented by the puritans – if you enjoy something, it has to be wrong. Some people get satisfaction out of being frugal, but if that isn't you, then don't deny yourself small pleasures in the belief that that's the way to wealth.

> ## CUTTING OUT YOUR DAILY CAPPUCCINO ISN'T GOING TO MAKE YOU RICH

Hang on though. Didn't I say in an earlier Rule that the rich are eagle-eyed and that you had to stop money leaks? Indeed. But that's different. While getting your finances in order is a good thing, going without isn't. Make sure you aren't giving money away by being careless (those are the leaks) but don't deny yourself the very small pleasures that enrich your life – just don't go mad. If you can't afford what you want, buy less, but buy quality. Save up by all means for those big purchases or ask if you really need them, but don't start thinking that giving up little luxuries, little treats, little life enhancers, will somehow increase your wealth. It won't. It will keep you trapped in the poverty cycle. Escaping from the poverty cycle and the penury mindset is your key to success, your path to prosperity.

Wealthy people don't scrimp and save. Sure some of them are quite tightfisted and you'd have to crowbar their wallets off them. But while they watch their money carefully, they don't cut the odd coffee or buy cheap jam in the hope it will make them more wealthy. It obviously won't.

Like being on a diet, if you deny yourself every small pleasure, you'll probably fail. Little indulgences are the way forward. Now who else is going to tell you that?

RULE 36

Real wealth comes from deals not fees

I'm not saying that it's impossible to become wealthy working for someone else, because it can happen (see the next Rule). And of course you have to define wealth, as we saw in Rule 2. It may be that you have no ambition to rival Bill Gates in the wealth stakes, but would be happy with a mortgage-free house, a couple of luxury holidays a year, and a good lump sum set aside for emergencies or to pass on to the kids. In that case selling your time, which is what you're effectively doing as an employee or a freelancer, may make you wealthy if you're sought after enough.

Look at the professional classes – they're a good example of what I mean. Lawyers and top doctors and successful financial advisers and so on. They all have extremely comfortable lives that many of us would aspire to. But they're none of them in the super-rich league – not unless they've either inherited their money, or they're doing something else on the side.

To make real, big, serious money you have to do deals. Buy and sell. I wasn't kidding when I told you in Rule 33 to learn the art of deal making. Because that's the only way to make millions. Look at the wealthiest people in the world – they're none of them employees, or even freelancers. They're all selling stuff. Computers, aeroplane seats, banking services, cars, newspapers.

Now hang on, don't jack in the day job just yet. I'm not saying you can't work for someone else, at least for now. But recognize that if your ambition is to make a fortune, you're going to have to leave the job eventually and strike out. Maybe you can wheel and deal on the side, and leave the job when you no longer need it. Or maybe you need a plan for setting up on your own. However you choose to play it, sooner or later you'll have to start buying and selling if you're going to become a millionaire.

YOU'LL HAVE TO START
BUYING AND SELLING IF
YOU'RE GOING TO BECOME
A MILLIONAIRE

RULE 37

Understand that working for others won't necessarily make you rich – but it might

Most of us assume that we'll never make it to greater prosperity while we are working for someone else; that only by being entrepreneurial will we become wealthy. And for a lot of us this may well be true – there is a limit as to how much you can earn per hour in return for your labour. However, there are some who do make it good this way.

We shouldn't overlook the fact that being employed may be the best route for us and that we don't have to run our own business. There are whole categories of employees that are doing quite nicely thank you. For example, a friend of mine works in corporate insurance and he's extremely wealthy thanks to large commission payments. He says he wouldn't be any better off working for himself.

Many people working in the computer business opted to become contractors because they assumed they would earn a lot more. Some did, but at the cost of stability. When the contracts dried up some were worse off than when employed. But for some this was indeed the best way to go and they have made handsome sums by becoming self-employed.

I guess you have to keep an open mind about this one and not be driven by assumptions. You can make yourself pretty unhappy by forcing yourself into self-employment if this isn't the right way for you. Perhaps the stability of employment is a greater priority and you should stick with it and not feel compelled to start your own business.

The converse is true as well: understand that working for yourself might make you rich, but it might not. Nearly two-thirds of business start-ups end in failure within three years. Look around you and you will see many examples of the small business owner struggling desperately. There's no certainty there. Working for yourself generally has higher earning potential, but not in every case. You have to look into it very closely – right business, right demand for your services, right time, enough effort and so on.

There isn't the space or time here to go into all the pros and cons of working for yourself. Except to say it's one hell of a lot easier and much more fun working hard for yourself than for someone else. But what we are aiming for isn't freedom from employment but prosperity. Hence we have to be open to whichever means will hasten our achievement of that goal. Employment or going it alone? It entirely depends on which one will get us rich easiest, fastest, slickest. And your day job doesn't have to be your route to wealth at all…

The secret is not to close your mind to any opportunity to get rich. And staying employed doesn't mean not having a little eBay business on the side or a buy-to-let property to create a new income stream.

> **PERHAPS THE STABILITY OF EMPLOYMENT IS A GREATER PRIORITY AND YOU SHOULD STICK WITH IT**

Don't waste time procrastinating – make money decisions quickly

If you are out at sea and it cuts up rough, you make for a safe harbour. Any port in a storm. You don't spend time procrastinating over whether the harbour has shower facilities or a branch of your favourite restaurant chain or cheaper moorings. No, you just get the hell out of the storm, while there's still space in the harbour, and be grateful it provides the one thing you really need – safety.

Making money is a bit like that. Sometimes you just need to act. As long as you get some return on your action, it's better than doing nothing. This isn't complicated but you'd be amazed how many people overlook this and think 'I'll decide how to invest that little lump sum I've saved up later – I can't decide whether to buy shares or put it in a savings account'. So they do nothing and the money sits in a current account earning no interest or, worse still, gets frittered away by default and inflation.

You don't have to think too deeply about this stuff. You don't have to think too hard. You don't even have to really think at all.

The samurai lived by a simple creed – no hesitation, no doubt, no surprise, no fear. It is simply the most brilliant strategy for doing anything. It basically says that once you have decided on a course of action (or battle or combat) then be committed; know everything you need to know about it, don't be afraid and get on with it as quickly as possible. If you've ever seen a samurai sword fight you'll notice they circle each other and then there is a dramatic burst of activity, a flurry of intense violence and it's all over. One or other or frequently both opponents are dead. The circling is not preparation – that was done over years and years of training. The circling is sussing out your opponent – taking their mind. When they go into attack it is a direct, swift, no hesitation attack. And your financial plans must have the same razor-sharp incisiveness about them.

> # THE SAMURAI LIVED BY A SIMPLE CREED – NO HESITATION, NO DOUBT, NO SURPRISE, NO FEAR

Doing something is invariably better than doing nothing – even if it's a firm decision to stay put. And sometimes acting fast can be a lot better than holding out on a possibility. Suppose you buy and sell antiques and collectables as a money-spinning hobby. If you buy a plate for £10 and think you can sell it for £30, but somebody offers you £20 within an hour, then you take the £20 and go and buy two more plates at £10 to sell on in the same way. I'm not saying you should act blindly – far from it. Like the samurai, we're talking about stuff you already know. Now you have to act on it. Make your decision wise and sensible and considered and thoughtful. But make it *now*. Quickly weigh up the odds, consider the pros and cons and then get on with it.

Work as if you didn't need the money

Most of us work because we *do* need the money. But some of us let it show and some of us don't. If somebody looks as though they don't need the money, it's for one of two reasons. Either (a) they put on a good act or (b) they genuinely enjoy their work and do it because they love it – they would do it even if they didn't need the money.

Clearly (b) is a fantastic place to be and one we should all strive to get to. But even if that's not the case for you yet, there's a very good reason to act as if you would work irrespective of the financial return. If people think (or indeed know) that you need the money, it gives them power over you and that puts you in a vulnerable position; it makes you insecure. If you work as if you don't need the money, they have no power and you have it instead.

> IF PEOPLE THINK THAT YOU NEED THE MONEY, IT GIVES THEM POWER OVER YOU AND THAT MAKES YOU INSECURE

Many years ago I worked in a job I hated and I was unhappy. Later on I started a business that my heart wasn't really in and it failed. But I have always written. Am I a writer? Not really. I don't write highbrow fiction. I wish I could but I know my limitations and stick to writing about what I see other people doing. But writing is something I have always done – whether I get paid for it or not. Whether it gets published or not. And that's my secret; I do it because I passionately care about it. It is my heart and soul and belief and drive and ambition. It is so much a part of me that no one can touch it or have power over it or take it away. Do you know how happy that makes me? Do you know how rich that is making me?* Do you know how much power that gives me?

So what's your secret? What makes your heart turn cartwheels? Where does your dream lie? You've got to be driven. Being prosperous has no room for 'I don't know' or 'I'm not sure'. You've got to know, you've got to be sure. Why? Because that is what wealthy people do. They know where they are going and what they are going to do when they get there. They have passion and drive and ambition and determination. They work because they want to.

Ah, but I hear you say, the passion and determination is something they are born with; it's in their personality. Perhaps it is. But it's also something you can emulate, copy, mirror. Do like them to become like them. Work as if you didn't need the money. Aim for the point where you don't do anything unless your heart is in it.**

---

* And for once I don't mean financially happy, although that too is part of it in a big way.
** Obviously, even if you are following your dream, there will be moments, days, when you've had enough and you're sick of everything... We're talking about what you overall enjoy, on the whole find pleasurable, mostly glory in.

Spend less than you earn

I'm amazed how many people flout this simple but most golden of all golden rules. You have to live within your means. Control your spending. Allow yourself to create a little bit of savings, with which to generate more income. (Remember the rabbit farm? You can't breed more rabbits if you sell them all.)

This Rule doesn't contradict Rule 35 about small economies not making you rich, by the way. You should live within your means but live well enough to be happy. If you don't earn enough to have champagne every week, then have it only once a month. But do have it if it makes you happy.

This is about being informed and in control. You need to know what your income is and what your outgoings are. We'll talk later about how to curb spending and make savings and how to cut up your credit cards if they've let you down – they do that sometimes, evil little things.

You also need to know:

- any expenditure that is likely to come up

- any provision you've made for contingency plans

- any future income you may be entitled to in the way of interest or investments coming to fruition.

And that really is about it. Where people go wrong is not whether they earn enough or spend too much – both of those are fairly easy to overcome. No, the biggest mistake is not knowing what you are doing, where you are financially and what is up ahead.

I know it can be tough to live within your means but if you are constantly in debt then all the prosperity that is rightfully yours is going to some faceless bank. I bet they're enjoying spending it. I bet they're having champagne more than once a week. Why encourage them?

I want you to know to the very week, the very hour, what you earn. And I want you to monitor what you spend, what it costs you to live – where you waste money, where you save money and where you spend money wisely. As long as more is coming in than is going out, you're getting the basics right. If more is going out than coming in, you need to take swift and effective action to redress the situation.

> # THE BIGGEST MISTAKE IS NOT KNOWING WHAT YOU ARE DOING, WHERE YOU ARE FINANCIALLY AND WHAT IS UP AHEAD

Don't borrow money – unless you really, really have to

This is so important that I will repeat it: don't borrow money unless you really, really have to. And even then don't. Not unless you are borrowing off someone who is lending it interest free, no strings, not secured against your house, no potential for messing up friendships – and that sounds like cloud cuckoo land. Ha, there is no such thing as free money (or a free lunch).*

If someone lends it, they'll want it back – plus. And that plus is what kills most of us, stops us from becoming prosperous. It has to be nipped in the bud. And if it's too late for that, then it needs to be severely pruned. We have to get rid of that plus.

The plus is usually financial (i.e. interest on the loan) and this is what usually cripples people. However, the plus can be emotional also – if you borrow from friends and family it can cause all kinds of other complications – it's never ever simple.

> ## IF SOMEONE LENDS IT, THEY'LL WANT IT BACK – PLUS

---

* There is such a thing actually – try putting 'freebies' into your search engine and you should find a free lunch somewhere.

Pay off your loans and debts before you do anything else. It's the only way to get rid of the plus. I know, I know, lots of people borrow money to start their own business and then go on to make millions and what am I talking about – we all have to borrow, don't we? Do we? I have a friend who started his own business with three friends. They all put in £500 and ran the business for 15 years. Then they sold it for £43 million. Yep, and not a penny borrowed. The upshot was they had to share with no one – and at times like this you don't want to share, no matter what your parents said about how we all should learn to share.

I have another friend who borrowed heavily to launch his business, which he successfully sold for £8 million. But nearly every penny of that went into loan repayments and interest. He was left with very little and, having not learnt his lesson, proceeded to start another business with capital raised by money loaned from the City. But he says he has learnt a lot because this time he's only borrowed £3 million. Ho ho.

When you are starting a business, advisers often say it's OK to borrow off people you know because they are willing to support you etc. But the novelist Jilly Cooper says she is wary of lending money to friends as it is terribly difficult to see someone at Christmas and give them a hug knowing they owe you £10,000. Personally I would find it hard to hug someone who owed me a lot less than that!

Try not to borrow from:

- your parents
- your children
- other people's children
- friends
- lovers
- passing strangers
- loan sharks
- the City
- banks
- credit card companies
- offshore investment bankers of any sort
- me.

Consider consolidating debts

Obviously the best advice is don't get into debt in the first place. If it's a bit late for that nugget of wisdom then you need to pay as little interest as you can while you are paying off your debts (which clearly you will be doing as quickly as possible). Consolidating debts is one way of doing this that might be right for you. What I am talking about here is stopping using three or four credit cards plus an overdraft plus a bank loan plus other borrowings. It is possible to consolidate all of them into one loan, tear up the cards (as if – you need industrial strength scissors, and here speaks a man who has cut up many a credit card) and pay off the overdraft. And yes I do understand the ease and usefulness of a credit card but don't forget that good old stand-by – cash.

A word of warning, however, if you do consolidate your debts: make sure you aren't turning short-term debts into long-term debts. The idea is strictly to pay off debt quickly.

> **DON'T FORGET THAT GOOD OLD STAND-BY – CASH**

If you do decide to consolidate your debts, here are some useful tips:

- I have a friend who wrote to all his creditors and offered them an immediate payment of 50 per cent if they would write the debt off – this included all his credit card people. Surprisingly every single one of them said yes and he took out a bank loan and paid them all off without having to declare himself bankrupt. He thus consolidated his debts and reduced them by half. Brilliant.

- Never ever respond to any adverts from companies offering to consolidate your debts for you – those ads are for people with more money than sense.

- Shop around for any pay-off loans – don't accept your bank's just because it is your bank: they may not be the cheapest by a long way.

- Don't secure anything against your home, ever, under any circumstances. If you do, you could lose your home if you don't keep up repayments. Is anything worth this risk? I don't think so.

- Check the small print regarding early settlements and make sure you aren't going to be penalized if you settle early.

- Only ever take out one loan to consolidate and only do this once – learn your lesson and move on.

- Pay off as quickly as you can afford – the longer the term, the more you'll have to pay in interest.

- If you must borrow, borrow against an asset you can resell (machine tool, delivery van) and try not to borrow more than the resale value.

- Buying on credit is a bit different. When Jack Cohen started Tesco he negotiated the rent for his shop to be paid three months in arrears, he paid for his stock three months in arrears, and started taking money over the counter on day 1. By day 90 he had taken a lot more than he owed.

RULE 43

Cultivate a skill and it'll repay you over and over again

There's a saying that he who pays the piper calls the tune. And that's true. But the piper can decide how much he will charge for playing that tune if what he plays is:

- in demand

- rare

- particularly difficult (or in some way unique) to play.

Get yourself a decent instrument, a decent set of tunes, an unusual or quirky PR approach, a USP,* create a name for yourself and the world will beat a path to your door. And pay you handsomely.

Once you can do something no one else can do – or as few people as is possible – you can pretty well name your price. And believe me it doesn't have to be a particularly difficult skill, just one that somebody else wants and will pay for. Remember the guy who polishes the very best cars at a premium price? (See Rule 8.)

You could train to be a brain surgeon** but it takes over ten years and aptitude and dedication and steady hands. So putting that aside, think about what you've got to offer. What are your skills, your talents, your strengths and weaknesses? Who needs those skills? How could you put them to best use? How do you tell the people who need these skills that you have them? What skill might you be able to master in order to meet a need that's out there waiting to be met?

---

* Unique selling proposition.
** Neurosurgeon, as they are properly titled.

> ONCE YOU CAN DO
> SOMETHING NO ONE
> ELSE CAN DO – OR AS FEW
> PEOPLE AS IS POSSIBLE –
> YOU CAN PRETTY WELL
> NAME YOUR PRICE

For this exercise you are not allowed to say:

- don't know

- not sure

- nothing really

- not a lot

- what do you mean? Talent? Skills? Me?

Come on, we all have something we can do or could do that is special to us, that we feel we could make a fortune from if only someone would give us a break.* We all have a dream we could follow, a plan we dare carry out. Perhaps all we need is a shove, a push in the right direction, a wake-up call to get up off our backside and actually do something. Well, this is it. WAKE UP. GET ON WITH IT.

---

* No one gives you a break – you create breaks. You go out there and wrestle breaks to the ground and beat them into submission, you lure them out of their caves with sweets on a stick, you track them down and hunt them with an opportunity gun, you stay in their face until they give in – but no one gives them away.

Pay off your loans and debts as a priority

Do you clear your credit card balance every month? If you do, and you don't have any other outstanding loans/debts then well done you. You're not wasting money paying interest and you're already in a strong position to go forward. Skip the rest of this Rule and carry on.

If you *do* have a credit card balance (or five), an overdraft and/or other loans or debts,* then you certainly aren't alone. We live in a 'have it now, pay later' society. Trouble is, debt bogs us down and holds us back. We're simply throwing money away paying off the interest (you borrow, say, £20,000 and can end up paying several thousand pounds extra back in interest – the actual amount you end up paying depends on how long you borrow for, as well as the interest rate you're being charged). Debt is a millstone round your neck – it makes you feel bad, it's always there nagging away at the back of your mind and it can easily become a major problem that affects your health as well as your wealth.

> **DEBT BOGS US DOWN**
>
> **AND HOLDS US BACK**

---

* We don't include mortgages in this category by the way – although strictly speaking it is a loan, it's an investment (we hope) and therefore is a special case.

There's no doubt about it. The very first thing you need to do on your wealth quest is to get loans/debts paid off as soon as possible and do nothing else until that's done. There's no point at all starting to put money into a savings account, earning say 5 per cent interest, if you are at the same time paying 10 per cent interest on money you owe to the bank or somebody else. It doesn't make any sense. The simple truth is that those who borrow almost always pay a higher rate of interest than the rate received by those who save.

I acknowledge that you may in fact have found a special situation where you can borrow money at a very low rate of interest and believe you can invest that money for a bigger return, but I say be very, very, very careful indeed. You are playing with fire here and unless the investment is absolutely risk free (which I doubt), pay the debt/loan off as fast as you possibly can.

I should stress here that there are a few possible special exemptions to this Rule; for example, if you've borrowed to invest in, say, a business and you really know what you're doing. We're really talking mainly about personal debt in this Rule.

I'm not playing down how difficult it is to become debt free, but it has to be done. Make a plan as to how you're going to get rid of your debt – start by paying off the highest interest debt first if you've more than one. Motivation is vital as this is short-term pain for long-term gain.

And of course once you finally make it to debt free, you're never going there again, are you? (See Rule 40.) Of course you aren't. You're a Rules Player now.

Don't be too busy earning a living to make some money

It's easily done. You needed a job because we all do, in order to live. Then you get into working for a living and it takes up such a huge amount of your time and energies that there's none left over to spend thinking about what you could be doing differently, extra or smarter in order to make more money. How many of us are guilty of letting our financial affairs slide because quite frankly we feel there are better things to do with our precious free time than get to grips with our finances or plan a long overdue life/career change?

Sometimes we're so busy doing our jobs, we forget the end goal – making some real money. Well, to become wealthy, you absolutely have to remember to lift your head above the parapet of your 9 to 5 (or 8 to 8 or whatever hours you work) and give yourself a chance to think about the bigger picture – and take action.

Lots and lots of people work to live – and without them the rich couldn't get richer. And this doesn't mean the workers are being exploited or used. Just that if people choose to be drudges and invest all their time and energy in working for wages, then there will always be other people who will be quick to see an opportunity and become prosperous, simply because they had their heads up and could see further.

If you do work for a living and don't confidently expect that job to make you rich, then you must be doing it for love, mustn't you? No, this isn't a trick question. It is about prioritizing our ambitions. If we go to work solely for money it makes sense to earn as much as we can, as we want.

If you love what you do then if the money doesn't come with it you need to create a strategy for wealth creation that doesn't rely on the 'day job' income. It's great that you love what you do, but if you also want wealth you need to make sure you aren't so busy doing it that you forget to work out how you're going to get wealthy doing it, or what other actions or strategies you need to create a second income or alternative revenue generator.

If you are unhappy with your pay and/or hate your job then you have to question why you're still doing it and what else you could do. The worst possible scenario is that you don't feel fulfilled or rewarded in your job but you are so busy doing it that you don't have time to create a plan that will bring you greater prosperity and happiness. While you've got your head down earning a living, a million and one opportunities to become prosperous have just passed over your head and you didn't see them. Imagine waking up in ten years' time and realizing that's what you'd done. If this is your situation then do something now. Change your perspective and seize the day.

> **IF WE GO TO WORK SOLELY FOR MONEY IT MAKES SENSE TO EARN AS MUCH AS WE CAN**

RULE 46

Save in big chunks – or should you?

I always thought that if I could get my hands on a big chunk I would put loads of it away and that would be a brilliant way of saving. I have a friend who says that is a nonsense and that the drip-by-drip effect is the best way to save. Who is right and who is wrong? Obviously I must be right. It's my book, after all.

Let us consider it a bit more logically. Suppose I save a big chunk. Let's say I get £20,000 for some work I do or something I sell. I spend half and save half. And I do this when I am 50. How much do I have at retirement?

My friend saves a measly, miserly £10 a month – small potatoes I say. But he does start early – at 20 and never misses a month. Who is going to retire big time and who is going to be reusing tea bags? Come on, come on, you can work this stuff out in your head, can't you? No? OK there's the chart opposite (assuming 5 per cent interest per annum).

See, I told you I was right...but not by much. Hope you have learnt a valuable lesson here. It's good to be prudent and save regularly but in the long run a big chunk saved later in life will bring home the bacon just as easily.

Year	My friend aged 20 at £10 per month	Me, who doesn't save a thing until I'm 50 – ha!
1	£126*	
2	£258	
3	£397	
4	£543	
5	£696	
6	£857	
7	£1,025	
8	£1,202	
9	£1,398	
10	£1,594	
11	£1,800	
12	£2,016	
13	£2,243	
14	£2,421	
15	£2,668	
16	£2,927	
17	£3,199	
18	£3,485	
19	£4,163	
20	£4,497	
21	£4,847	
22	£5,215	
23	£5,601	
24	£6,007	
25	£6,433	
26	£6,880	
27	£7,350	
28	£7,843	
29	£8,361	
30	£8,905	This is the year I make my big savings killing with £10,000 + 5% = £10,500**
31	£9,476	£11,025
32	£10,075	£11,576
33	£10,704	£12,154
34	£11,365	£12,761
35	£12,059	£13,399
36	£12,787	£14,068
37	£13,552	£14,771
38	£14,355	£15,509
39	£15,198	£16,284
40	£16,083	£17,098
41	£17,013	£17,952
42	£17,989	£18,849
43	£19,014	£19,791
44	£20,090	£20,780
45	£21,220	£21,819
Totals	£21,220	£21,819

* I know, I know, he won't get 5 per cent on the whole lot because he won't have the full £120 until the end of year 1 but this is just an example.

** I'm assuming I invest at the beginning of the year.

RULE 47

Don't rent, buy

We all need somewhere to live. We therefore have the choice as to whether to rent the roof over our heads, or buy it. Most of us can't afford to buy outright (I doubt you'd be reading this book if you were in this category), so in order to buy we need to borrow a lump sum of money to buy with. But hang on. Haven't we said that borrowing is bad, bad, bad and we shouldn't do it? Haven't we said that this way madness lies because you pay so much interest on what you borrow and so on? Indeed we have.

So how can you own and not borrow, buy and not have a mortgage?

The answer is that a mortgage can actually be viewed as an investment rather than a borrowing. If you buy a property with a mortgage, you make a monthly investment. The fact you pay that to a mortgage company we can gloss over. You see, in the longer term (and if you're lucky, the shorter term too) you can reasonably expect that the interest you pay on your mortgage will be less than the increase in the value of your property. What you are banking on is that the value of your home will, in the longer term, go up and therefore you have invested whatever deposit you put down, and your mortgage money.

> ## SO HOW CAN YOU OWN AND NOT BORROW, BUY AND NOT HAVE A MORTGAGE?

Renting on the other hand is not an investment. You will never see that money again. Of that there is no doubt.

With a mortgage, you stand a good chance in the long term of seeing your mortgage payments lead to an increase in the value of your house. When you sell, you get that increase in value. Bear in mind, however, that buying property is a long-term investment and you may not gain in the short term. If property prices plummet, you'll struggle to turn any of your asset into cash. Some experts advise that your house should represent only half of your total assets. That might seem optimistic to some of us, but it's a good target to aim for.

There are those who believe that buying your home instead of renting brings with it huge stresses, and means you have less fun. The lesson is to think carefully about how much your mortgage repayments will be and whether you are able and willing to pay them.

Ideally buy cheap and sell for a lot more. You then have a choice. You can invest the profits in the next property without borrowing any more and in doing so you decrease the mortgage each time. Eventually you own outright, without mortgage payments, and you have somewhere to live and don't have to pay for it at all any more.

Alternatively you can do what most people do and buy a bigger, better, more expensive house. This isn't a wealth creation strategy but it can be what you wanted your wealth for, which makes it fine by me.

Understand what investing really means

Many investments have a twofold purpose. They generate income and they increase in value. In other words, if you invest a lump sum (this is known as capital) you get regular small payments of some kind *and* the actual value of the capital itself increases, i.e. the lump sum gets bigger.

Let's suppose you invest in property. In an ideal world you should be able to rent it out, thus providing the regular small payments in the form of rental income, and the value of the property should go up also, so your capital increases in value over time.

Likewise shares should pay out dividends (generate income) and should be worth more than you bought them for when you come to sell some time later (increase in value). You get the idea. And notice I say 'should' rather than 'will' – nothing is certain in this game.

You can of course invest in pretty well anything you want:

* company shares
* your brother's harebrained buy-an-old-boat-and-do-it-up-and-sell-it-for-a-fortune scheme
* fine wines, paintings, krugerrands, classic cars, rare books, Georgian glass
* pension funds and such like including savings and deposit accounts
* inventions and new product development
* ideas and people
* theatre shows, films, TV programme development.

And it doesn't have to be just plain old investment. There is also:

- sponsorship such as race cars, football teams etc. to raise brand awareness (hopefully yours and not just the race car or football team)

- angelic capital – you invest in people and ideas in an altruistic way rather than purely as a money-making venture (as opposed to venture capital, where you invest in people and ideas purely as a money-making venture).

Remember that investments of any sort are a form of gambling no matter which way you look at it. And that you can lose. Ask Lloyd's if you don't believe me.

On the other hand, investing in a broad range of low-risk investments can still net returns worth having.

REMEMBER THAT INVESTMENTS OF ANY SORT ARE A FORM OF GAMBLING NO MATTER WHICH WAY YOU LOOK AT IT

Build a bit of capital then invest it wisely

Lots of people don't get prosperous because, as we saw earlier, they are too lazy. But a lot fail because they don't know what to do once they start to earn some money. It's easy to think, once you've got your hands on a bit, that you have earned it, you deserve it, you're going to spend it. You *have* earned it – assuming you haven't robbed anyone to get it – and yes you probably *do* deserve it. But no, don't spend it all now, no matter how much you want that new car, holiday, cottage by the sea, whatever.

I've done it. I guess we all have. I once got a massive tax rebate. I don't remember why I was being taxed so highly but I was for several years and when they repaid me it was quite a handsome sum. And of course I blew it, on a spendid holiday. But that's the difference between the rich and the not so well-off. The rich see a sudden windfall like that as an opportunity to make some more money out of it. The not so well-off remain not so well-off as they see it as an opportunity to have some fun. Nothing wrong with that if that's what you want in life – instant pleasure. But if you want greater wealth and pleasure (albeit delayed) then you must learn as I did that once you get your hands on a lump sum, or build some up, you must immediately put it to good use. And frankly the only good use is as a starter kit for prosperity.

And it isn't lost, merely put to one side to work for you. Once it has grown and attracted lots more lovely money, you can have all the holidays you want. But you have to wait and you have to use that starter kit well and wisely. See it as a 'loader'. This is a term guides who receive tips use for starting the tip collection off. You have to put a loader in the plate or no one else will tip. Buskers do the same thing, put a coin or two into the hat to get the crowd going. No one will put anything into an empty hat. What you are going to do is load your prosperity hat.

Ah, but I hear you say, I'm never going to get my hands on a lump sum. Not true. You get your hands on a lump sum every week of your life in the form of wages – I'm assuming you do have a job here. You choose what you spend that money on – mortgage, food, car, entertainment, etc. But if you want a way out of that particular lifestyle and into another, you have to be proactive about it. And the way you start it is to put something aside each week to build up that lump sum. Once you have something built up, think about where that money is going to generate you more money, and get it invested. Ideally you need to turn that money into an asset that will generate more revenue for you – be it shares, a property you can rent out, or something else. Wealth happens slowly over a period of time, when you turn surplus cash into something that will work for you.

> # NO ONE WILL PUT ANYTHING
> # INTO AN EMPTY HAT

RULE 50

Understand that property, in the long run, will not outpace shares

So, you've built up a bit of money to invest – where to put it? Property and shares are two popular choices, but which to choose?

In the aftermath of the 'dot com' crash of 2000 when share prices started to plummet, many people in the UK turned from investing in shares to investing in property. It's not surprising really – many people who invested heavily in shares in the late 1990s saw the value of many of those shares drop so much it really hurt – and some companies folded completely, meaning investors lost all their money.

With people turning in huge numbers from shares to property, the buy-to-let market boomed and with greater demand from investor buyers, house prices rose. Eventually we reached a point where in some areas there was a glut of property available to rent and income from rental properties failed to match expectations (supply outstripping demand). However, those early into the buy-to-let boom who bought in the right areas did well. In the years since 2000, however, share prices have recovered and those who could hold on to their shares on the whole have seen their value climb again.

So what's the right thing to do? Property or shares? Well, shorter-term blips notwithstanding, in the longer run, shares will outperform property.

Don't get me wrong – there's always a place for property – it's about getting yourself a good spread of investments – a portfolio as the professionals like to call it. Any decent investment portfolio is going to include property as a matter of course.

One big advantage of investing in property is that you can live in it (as we said in Rule 47, you have to live somewhere and you can't live in cocoa futures). Alternatively, if you're buying to let, you will get income from the rental of the property (though you have to be extremely careful that the rent is as much as you hope it will be, that you are sure there is enough demand for rental properties in that area, and so on).

With shares, you hope to get regular income in the form of dividends paid to shareholders, but the greatest return usually comes from a long-term increase in share prices. And quite simply, as companies have greater potential for growth than property, the longer-term picture should see shares giving you a greater return. I stress potential here as it doesn't always get realized – the value of your shares, or your property, can go down as well as up. There's always risk. The other reason to prefer shares to property alone is that shares – especially a nice well-balanced portfolio – will give you a decent risk spread. The more variety, the less the risk. Did you know that in a slump baked bean sales go up?

> **ANY DECENT INVESTMENT PORTFOLIO IS GOING TO INCLUDE PROPERTY AS A MATTER OF COURSE**

Master the art of selling

Just as deal making is a vital skill, so is selling – and they aren't always the same thing. You sell stuff outside of deals. Indeed one of the most important things you have to be able to sell in life to increase your prosperity is yourself.

Selling is the bedrock upon which every fortune is built. Whatever you do to make yourself prosperous will involve selling: selling your skills, selling things, selling ideas. You can't make money without selling. Selling is where it's at. Every rich person knows this simple fact. Every poor person doesn't.

In an ideal world you should aim to sell:

- yourself and your abilities, skills and attributes (every minute of every day)

- something while you're asleep

- in countries you've not only never been to but have never heard of

- via other people, so someone else is selling for you

- things that are incredibly cheap to produce and give you a really healthy return

- things other people make and finance for you

- things that have a 99 per cent penetration into every household

- things that store, transport and stack easily.

The list is probably endless. But where people go wrong is when they try to sell things that no one really wants. Unless of course you are Damien Hirst and you make pickled sharks. Now there's a market I never thought of.

And don't go thinking selling is for sales reps in shiny suits with a nice line in patter. Every time Richard Branson appears on television busy with a hot air balloon he is selling; selling his entire brand. Clever man. Clever selling.

I like the young chap Alex Tew who started at university in 2005. He wanted to become a millionaire and realized that if he had a million things he could sell them all for $1 and achieve his goal. And he realized a web page has 1 million pixels. He then set about selling each one for $1 to advertisers. You need a block of around 400 (thus costing $400) to be seen, but he sold half by Christmas and the rest within his first year at uni. Head down? I don't think so. You can see the result at www.milliondollarhomepage.com – and yes, I supported his venture and paid him $400 for advertising my business as I figured such an enterprising young man needed a monetary round of applause for ingenuity, cleverness and innovation.

> # SELLING IS THE BEDROCK UPON WHICH EVERY FORTUNE IS BUILT

RULE 52

See yourself as others do

If your plan towards wealth means you're going to sell anything – your time, your products, your services or anything else – you need to be the kind of person people want to buy from. If you want to be seriously wealthy, you'll need to think about yourself and how you come across very hard and very honestly. You'll need to know how other people see you, and if necessary adapt your image to suit your line of business.

Would you buy a pension from someone wearing torn jeans, a hoodie and flip-flops, and chewing gum? No indeed. Would you sign up for surf lessons from someone in a three-piece suit and a comb-over? Of course not. But swap these two round...now we're talking.

And it's not just about the way you dress of course. It's about your personality, your manner, your attitude, your punctuality, your integrity, your communication skills, your level of organization, the car you drive, whether you hold your meetings over breakfast or with a drink down the pub, how open and honest you are, whether your paperwork is efficient, scary or non-existent, how fast you return phone calls, whether you market yourself aggressively or subtly, whether you're arrogant or self-effacing, what you promise and whether you make people laugh. And more.

Every aspect of your 'brand' should be conscious and considered. Don't leave it to chance. Ask friends (who you trust to be honest) to tell you how you come across, and listen to feedback from colleagues and work contacts too – whether it's direct or implied. They might not be totally honest of course – get ready to read between the lines.

And whatever you do you must be sincere too, because that will show. No, it's not difficult because you shouldn't be constructing an entirely artificial personality – you're just making sure that you've got the right skills (easy to talk to, good with numbers, or whatever) and then you make sure you show the bits of your own, genuine, personality that people want to see. If you're having trouble with this, what on earth are you doing in the job?

I have very dear friends, a couple, who are among the funniest people I know. They amuse me endlessly with their sharp-witted, slightly subversive humour. Evenings spent with them are always hilarious. Their job? They're funeral directors. When they're at work, they hide their sense of humour unless their clients clearly appreciate it. But another aspect of their personalities shines through – their caring, thoughtful, compassionate side. That's just as honest and genuine a part of them. It simply isn't the whole story.

> ## MAKE SURE YOU SHOW THE BITS OF YOUR OWN PERSONALITY THAT PEOPLE WANT TO SEE

RULE 53

Don't believe you can always win

There is a whole list of things and people you can't beat, so it might be best to be cautious around them. They include the bookies (and anyone else trying to take money off you for gambling – casino owners, card sharps, race courses, online gambling websites etc.), the tax authorities, speed cameras, the government, your mother, planning authorities, the police, your kids and death.

Dan Brown, author of *The Da Vinci Code*, was sued by the authors of another book, *Holy Blood, Holy Grail*, as they believed he had plagiarized their work. They lost. They lost big time. They lost somewhere in the region of £1.75 million including costs.

They probably believed quite sincerely in the merits of their case, but did anybody tell them they were unlikely to win? It'd be fascinating to know whether anybody advised them not to proceed as they would probably lose...

The reason to be very cautious in your dealings with bookies, barristers, accountants and such like is that they have knowledge you don't. They are holders of secrets that can enable them (if they so choose) to make money out of you purely because of your ignorance.

And don't go getting all moralistic on me and trying to change the system. These are facts of life. Live with them. Work with them. You won't get rid of them. You can't beat the bookies – or the odds – so don't go trying or attempting to get rid of them on the grounds that they are making money out of the poor, innocent and gullible public. Trouble is, the poor, innocent, gullible public walk in there with their wallets open, crying

'Help yourself'. And then complain they are broke, no one gives them a chance, life isn't fair, no one likes me, it's not my fault, there ought to be a law against it, etc. Remember that there are sharks out there. So don't bleed.

> **REMEMBER THAT THERE ARE SHARKS OUT THERE. SO DON'T BLEED**

Don't pick stocks yourself if you don't know what you're doing

The Rule after this one is about investing in the stock market. But before you go there, I should just point out that the next Rule may not apply to you at all. You might be better off skipping it altogether. If you don't really, truly, know what you're doing, you shouldn't be playing the stock market. Basically this Rule is about whether or not you should read the next Rule.

It's all very well saying that no one should invest in the stock market unless they know what they're doing. How on earth can you do it for the first time then? Isn't it like having a baby or sky-diving – you just have to learn as you do it? Well, yes and no. You see there are people who know what they are doing, and I guess they weren't born knowing what to do, so it must be possible to learn before doing so you are as prepared as possible.

So, you want to learn about stocks and shares. But how are you going to do it without getting your fingers burnt? It's actually very easy. Of course, you can do all the usual things like read the financial pages, talk to people who know more about it than you, ask advice, watch relevant TV programmes, buy books on the subject. Go ahead – you'll find all these things invaluable. But even so, how can you be completely certain you've really understood everything you've read and heard and learnt?

Dummy runs, that's how. Decide exactly where you're going to put your money … and then don't do it. Watch the markets. See what happens to your imaginary investments. Track their progress. Decide when to sell – and then see what happens to the price.

Write all this down – it's far too easy to tell yourself you predicted something when actually you merely noted the possibility of it happening but weren't sure if it would. Note down what you buy and when you sell and what you predict and how much money your initial imaginary investment would have gained (or lost) you.

Do this a lot. Not just one dummy run but plenty. Follow lots of companies, and keep doing it for months or years. Calculate your hit rate, your losses, your accuracy. And then, when your notes can prove on paper that you really do know what you're doing – that's when you can start investing for real. And even so, keep it small to begin with. It's not the same when you're 'playing' with real money and you may unconsciously modify your strategies, so carry on keeping those notes and records and don't let yourself get carried away.

DECIDE EXACTLY WHERE YOU'RE GOING TO PUT YOUR MONEY . . . AND THEN DON'T DO IT

RULE 55

Understand how the stock market *really* works

It's simple. People buy, sell and trade investments – called stocks – that they have made in companies. So, how does it all work? And, more importantly, *what* works?

The easy answer to the last question is 'Buy low; sell high', but don't you just know that there's more to it than that. The question of deciding what to buy, how much to pay for it and when to buy (and then sell) has been the subject of entire libraries of books, most of them bigger than this one, and so I'll limit my contribution to a few choice rules. The first of these is to understand the real forces at play: value and speculation.

Personally, I think economists were put on this earth to make astrologers look good, but I'm not averse to quoting them, and one of the most quotable – John Maynard Keynes – once said that the stock market is just like a beauty contest.

Now when he said that, he didn't mean that stockbrokers should abandon their suits for swimwear and profess a desire for working with children or world peace. He was referring to a type of British beauty contest that used to be run by London newspapers, in which readers could win a prize by picking the beauty whose photograph was deemed to be the most beautiful by the greatest number of other readers. This meant that winning was not about picking the prettiest, nor even about predicting which the average reader would think the prettiest, but instead winning became a game of anticipating what the average reader would expect the average choice to be. And this, believed Keynes, was how the stock market works. Investors try to make money by buying stocks that they think other investors will want to buy in the future, and the price that they're prepared to pay for a stock depends less on the fundamental value of the company than on their expectations of what everybody else will be willing to pay for it. That's the essence of speculation in the stock market, and that's why the fundamental value of a stock and its price on any given day can be so different.

Speculating on stock market movements is great fun if you want to observe mass psychology in action, but in an uncertain world it's not the road to wealth. And it's riskier than you realize unless you really know what you're doing. So don't start playing the game until you're sure you understand the rules. But if you really want to accumulate wealth in the stock market, then here's my advice. Get rich slowly, but surely, with value. Ignore all the noise, the clamour about what this piece of news or that piece of gossip means for a price; stay away from the 'proven' techniques for predicting what prices will do tomorrow based on what they did yesterday (technical analysis – don't be fooled by the rational-sounding label, it's irrational) and resist, please resist, the temptation to dive in and out of stocks chasing a quick buck. If you're going to invest in shares, look for value. Look for companies whose share price doesn't reflect their worth; look for companies that make or do something that people will find more valuable in the future; and look for companies whose value is appreciated by the investment funds (we'll meet them in Rule 56).

Once you've found them, buy them and, unless the fundamentals change, buy them for the long run. Wait for their value to appreciate, and watch as your wealth accumulates.

So, to buy the right stocks, at the right price of course, don't follow the crowd, find the value. Easier said than done, you might say, and you'd be right. It can take a lot of research, but you can make it easier if you follow the next Rule.

RULE 56

Only buy shares (or anything) you can understand

This is another Rule to engrave on your heart. Buying shares – or anything else to sell on in order to make money – is just another form of gambling. When I worked as a casino manager, it was well recognized that there was a hierarchy of casinos. At the bottom were the ones with the slot machines and noisy brash atmosphere. At the top were the gentlemen's clubs where it was all smoked glass and diffused lighting. Gamblers of course recognized the hierarchy and felt that the latter were somehow 'cleaner'. Similarly most people view the stock market as in some way more refined, sophisticated – and thus free of risk or odds or danger. But it is all gambling. Nothing is certain.

If you are going to gamble on shares (or anything else you want to buy and sell), then reduce the odds as much as possible and only invest in or buy things you know and understand. By doing this you eliminate a lot of the mystique which can lead you to stake more than you intend, take risks you wouldn't normally, or be bamboozled by slick marketing spiel.

If you shop at Marks & Spencer, and you see that the new product ranges are good and that the stores are full and you hear people raving about how M&S has improved this year, then buy M&S shares. If you keep studying the stores and listening to people shopping you will quickly notice if it continues to be a good investment.

REDUCE THE ODDS AS MUCH AS POSSIBLE AND ONLY INVEST IN OR BUY THINGS YOU UNDERSTAND

Just be careful you are aware whether you are buying with your head or heart. I have a friend who only invests in green companies. He swans about with an air of moral superiority. He believes he has bought a ticket to heaven by doing this. He is a gambler. He doesn't realize this. Is he buying with his head as well as his heart? If you find investments in something you love, be clear if you are buying as an investment on business principles, or simply because you want to. If your rational market analysis says that wind farms are the future, and will be a growing industry with big returns, then fantastic, you can invest with head and heart.

If you don't really understand a particular sector of business, and don't intend to put the work in to get to know it well, then you'll almost certainly be better off investing in something else. If you want to invest in shares, but don't want to do all the homework and make all the decisions yourself, then you can use an investment fund (see Rule 58).

Use your head

The reason you're reading this book is because you want to become wealthy, right? All the financial decisions you make will be geared towards generating as much money as possible. Each step along the way is just that – one more step on your wealth ladder.

So don't allow yourself to get distracted into making decisions on any other basis than their financial merit. Make sure your head rules your heart. That's probably not difficult if you're picking shares to invest in, but it can be hard when you're buying property, for example, or if you want to buy and sell old cars or antiques or anything you have a personal affection for.

I'm not saying you can't buy things you like – you have to decide how much of your wealth you want to enjoy and how much you'll save for later. But where a transaction is intended as an investment, when your primary purpose is to make money, don't allow yourself to be swayed by personal taste. If that beautiful old Series 1 Land Rover needs more work before you can sell it on than the newer Defender, and will fetch no more money at the end of it, then buy the Defender. It's tough I know, but it has to be done.

> **DON'T MAKE DECISIONS ON ANY OTHER BASIS THAN THEIR FINANCIAL MERIT**

Similarly if you're buying an investment property, such as a buy-to-let, don't choose a house just because it's in an area you'd like to live in. You're not the one who'll be living there, so you need to base your decision on hard financial factors, not your own preference. Which property will give you the best return (after costs)? That's all you need to know.

Look, I'm not telling you what you should and shouldn't do on a personal level. I'm just explaining how to get wealthy. That's what you asked me, in effect, when you bought this book, and that's what I'm telling you. The people who get wealthiest are the people who buy with their heads and not their hearts. So you do what you like, but don't say I didn't tell you.

RULE 58

By all means, use the investment professionals (but don't be used by them)

As you've probably guessed from Rule 55, most of those who pick their own stocks like to think that they can see value where others can't. Of course, we don't like to look too often to see if our track record backs that up, and I'm sure many a Rules Player has made dumb investment decisions. If you don't trust yourself to make clever decisions every time, or perhaps simply want to save the occasional investment decision for yourself and let someone who knows more than you do take care of the rest, then it's OK to use the professionals. But make sure you use them wisely.

Now, pay attention to this bit – it's really, really important. First, professionals will tell you that they can take your money, invest it actively and beat the market. That they do beat the market and that they will beat the market. They may even have some colourful charts to show you how they beat the market, every year. Apart from last year of course (and that was just a blip, a short-term correction you know, everybody took a bath on that one, but next year...). Just sign here, sit back and you'll soon be worth more than Warren Buffett on a hot streak. Sounds too good to be true? Yep, it's wishful thinking and flawed logic in equal measures.

To put it simply, for somebody to be doing better than average, somebody else must be doing worse, and since the big firms invest most of the money in the market, who are they beating? Themselves? Right, and here's the ugly little truth about the investment industry. In any given year, some will come out ahead and some will lose, but over the long term the market beats most of them, most of the time. Oh I'm sure many of them try hard, they really do, but in the end nearly all of them fail to grow money any faster than the market. So, don't pay them for trying.

Ask yourself this. If, like most people, you read the brochure, listen to the adviser (who's on a commission) and buy into a fund aiming to beat the market, what's the one thing that you can be sure will be higher than average? The returns? Or the fees? You know the answer to that one, don't you?

If you want help to put your money in the markets, without putting much of it in someone else's pockets, keep it simple.

If you don't have the time or know-how to carefully research the best active fund then follow the rule that less is more (and usually comes cheaper). Put your trust in funds that don't charge you big fees for taking big risks with a succession of clever strategies to beat the house – pick index funds and tracker funds. Pick funds managed by people who'll invest your money with minimum fuss and minimum fees, in a good range of stocks that replicate the market, and then go to lunch. Then you can sleep at night (or get back to reading this book) safe in the knowledge that your money is in the market, quietly working away on your behalf.

> **IN THE END MOST OF THEM FAIL TO GROW MONEY ANY FASTER THAN THE MARKET. SO, DON'T PAY THEM FOR TRYING**

RULE 59

If you are going to get financial advice, pay for it

Boy, are there a lot of people out there waiting and wanting to give you financial help, advice, information, tips and guidance. Great – learn early on to be very careful who you take advice from if you want to hang on to your wealth.

There are two groups of people to whom you may turn in the event of needing said advice, help, guidance, whatever. First, there are skilled professionals who carry indemnity insurance so you can sue them – and expect to get a payout – in the unlikely event the information they give you is erroneous, wrong, or dangerously bad. If they stand by their advice, you should make sure provision is there so that you get paid if it is wrong. That keeps 'em on their toes. These people you pay and their fee entitles them to talk to you about your money.

Second, there are very rich people. Listen to them, unless they won their money on the lottery, inherited it, robbed a bank to get it or bought a load of drugs in Marrakech and sold them in the local nightclub (actually their entrepreneurial skills might be worth something even if their honesty or honour isn't).

Those are the only two categories open to you. The ones closed to you include: friends and family, well-meaning acquaintances (even if they do have a quid or two of their own), TV programmes, the internet and high street banks.

You must make sure any financial advice comes from someone who carries a recognizable qualification or membership of a suitable organization – that includes the very, very rich club. Make sure you know that they know what they are doing.

The textile millionaire Joe Hyman used to say that in order of honesty, the three types of bank were high street banks, mountebanks and merchant banks.

There are two types of advisers in my experience: (a) those who stop you making an ass of yourself and (b) those who tell you you've made an ass of yourself after you've done it. You want category (a). You'll get loads and loads in category (b).

When it comes to professional financial advisers, there are another two categories: (a) those who deal with your finances and (b) those who try to sell you products. Avoid (b) like the plague.

Any financial adviser you use should be independent – i.e. they should not be restricted to providing advice from a limited range of products offered by the company they work for. It's the difference between buying a suit off the peg – a best fit – or buying something tailor-made to fit your requirements precisely.

MAKE SURE ANY FINANCIAL ADVICE COMES FROM SOMEONE WHO CARRIES MEMBERSHIP OF A SUITABLE ORGANIZATION – THAT INCLUDES THE VERY, VERY RICH CLUB

Don't fiddle

Once you've worked out a strategy, leave it alone. There is no point fiddling, you're unlikely to make it any better, and you might make it worse. Not only that but you could incur lots of extra charges or penalties if you start changing things after a short time. You have to know when to leave things alone. It's like the proverb: 'Look before you leap'. Look, look long and hard. Then make your plan and take your decisions. Then leave it alone – don't mess with it.

Looking is weighing up the odds, seeking advice, considering the pros and cons. Leaping is acting on all that information. But once you have decided to leap, get on with it. Once you have formulated your plan, your objective, your strategy, your goals and targets and ambitions and destinations, then be committed.

It is so easy to get scared or panicky. We all fear unemployment, poverty, financial traps, falling behind, falling below, falling in debt. I've been there: paralyzed by fear into staying in a job for years because I didn't believe I could survive outside it. Once I stepped outside, I survived just fine. We always do.

Plans and small fish require the same amount of cooking. Once they're in the pan, leave them alone or they'll fall apart. Don't keep stirring or they'll disintegrate. Don't keep fiddling, tinkering, changing your mind and changing it back again. If you do keep on fiddling you may end up achieving very little and worse still you will have frittered and wasted money on early redemption charges and the like. Many investments are long term and fiddling means paying more or not reaping the full benefits.

Sure you should keep your eye on things, and on the market generally, but stick with your strategy and, having done your homework, leave as well alone as possible. Don't panic and don't fiddle.

> **ONCE YOU HAVE DECIDED TO LEAP, GET ON WITH IT**

RULE 61

Think long term

At the same time as not fiddling too much (see Rule 60), so too you shouldn't play the short game. You have to think long term, both in your planning, and in your expectations of a return. You also have to invest for the longer term.

If you expect a rapid and sudden catapult into prosperity then go play the lottery and good luck to you (you'll need it). Gaining wealth is a slow process and rightly so. If you get it all quickly you have no time to acquire experience and sense. Too quickly and it'll be all 'spend, spend, spend'.

Thinking long term is a bit like thinking in very fast motion while the rest of the world moves incredibly slowly around you. 'Softly, softly catchee monkey', as they say. Ever tried to swat a fly? A fly's eyes are different from ours and they basically see in fast forward. By the time you raise your hand, they have already predicted the movement and flown away. You have to develop the same ability. You have to see what's happening before it happens and the only way to do that is to think long term.

Think of gaining prosperity as stalking a reluctant tiger. It'll be wary and cautious and you have to stalk it skilfully, quietly, almost lovingly. It's no use running up and shouting at it – it will either turn round and kill you or run off. Better to take your time and creep up slowly and quietly. Any sudden movements will startle the canny beast.

In *The Rules of Work* I talked about having various plans in force – short-term, medium-term and long-term. The same is true for investments. You need short-term investments for money you might need access to in the near future; medium-term ones that you expect to deliver returns in five or ten years say; and then you need long-term investments that will reap greater rewards but that deliver in the more distant future.

THINK OF GAINING PROSPERITY AS STALKING A RELUCTANT TIGER

I know in Rule 38 I said to be decisive and act quickly, and that is still true. But only after you have taken a long-term view; only after you have weighed and considered and pondered and evaluated. *The samurai only makes one cut but that cut was an entire lifetime in the making.*

Where are you going to be in five years' time, prosperity-wise? Ten? Fifteen? Twenty? Longer?

RULE 62

Have a set time of day to work on your wealth strategy

You have to have a life as well as gaining prosperity. It is my observation that happy, wealthy people's financial planning follows a similar set of four principles:

1 They set targets then get on with it.

2 They don't tinker too much.

3 They tend to work on their financial planning at the same time of day. (I don't mean everyone works at say 9am but that each person tends to favour a particular time of day whether it's 10.30 in the morning or midnight.)

4 They are able to take a break from their financial planning and have a life outside it – it keeps them refreshed and interesting.

The reason you need a set time of day is twofold. Firstly, it makes sure you actively manage your wealth rather than looking at it once a year and thinking 'Oh dear', and conversely it means you don't overdo it and spend all day tinkering (which as we've said is a bad idea). And secondly, it means you can take advantage of your natural biorhythms and put in the effort when you are at your brightest. If you are a morning person, you'll want to get your planning in early. If you are more of an owl, then an evening slot will take advantage of your sharpest mental acuity.

The other big advantage of having a set time of day is that you can plan for it, work it into your diary and make time for it. If you don't, it can get forgotten or the time is used for other things. If, for example, you always spend half an hour on your plan first thing after breakfast, then it gets to be a regular function and one you feel oddly uncomfortable missing – yes, even on holiday.

Working on your prosperity plan at the same time of day – and for the same shortish length of time – means you can break things down into manageable chunks and not get overwhelmed. You can work for a bit and then take a break, put it behind you for the day and go back to it, at the same time of course, the next day. Bit by bit, things will improve. Believe me, I've been here before you.

> # BIT BY BIT, THINGS
> # WILL IMPROVE

Pay attention to detail

This is my biggest failing I'm afraid. My solution is easy. I employ someone to manage my life who takes care of the detail – someone who is very, very good at the detail. Yes, it's an expensive way to do it. Better to train yourself right from the word go to pay attention to the detail yourself and save the expense.

Detail is not keeping a note of every tiny purchase you make and looking at minute economies – we've already discovered (see Rule 35) going without that cappuccino isn't going to make you rich beyond your wildest dreams. Detail is:

- checking the small print

- checking the interest rates

- checking charges and fees

- checking you pay for things on time so you don't incur penalties

- checking when you will be paid and that you invest promptly to avoid your money lying idle

- not forgetting people

- not forgetting dates, times and appointments

- making lists and writing everything down

- remembering to ask for information

- remembering to ask questions in general

- remembering to keep good records of all transactions, purchases and sales.

This is just muscle training. I take it you know all about muscle training? When you are in training for any sport, if you repeat an action often enough your muscles retain the memory of that action. The more you repeat the action the easier it gets and the less effort you need to put in.

It's a bit like driving a car, tough at first but it becomes automatic (excuse pun!) after a while. I am writing this in France and I have been getting used to (a) driving on the right and (b) driving a left-hand-drive car. I've had to concentrate hard and shout at the children because I can't think if they are beating seven bells out of each other in the back seat. It's been a bit like learning to drive all over again. Added to the fact that all the signs are in French and it's a steep learning curve. But it's getting easier and becoming routine. I don't have to think about it any more and can take in the passing scenery and enjoy the journey.

TRAIN YOURSELF RIGHT FROM THE WORD GO TO PAY ATTENTION TO THE DETAIL YOURSELF

Create new income streams

When it comes to wealth-creation strategies, investing wisely and managing your money actively are important, but nothing beats having more coming in in the first place. Everybody benefits from some thought about where their income comes from and how they could create another source of revenue.

It's a bit like being a busker and having several pitches. If one is proving unprofitable, you can pack it in and go somewhere else. But instead of packing it in, what you are going to do is duplicate yourself – a cloned you if you like – and not only carry on busking but also be busking in a new place at the same time. The more hats you have out, the more they are likely to return a profit.

Look, don't take my word for this. Check it out yourself. Look at any prosperous person you admire and see if diversity isn't their tool for unlocking greater prosperity. The rich usually have several money-making schemes going for them.

This is especially important for anybody who loves their work, but it doesn't pay well. What you need is another income stream.

There are a couple of ways of doing this. The first is to turn surplus cash into assets that will work for you and bring in income, even when you aren't there. Rent from a buy-to-let property would be one example, or annual dividends from shares you've bought.

The other way to create new income streams is to find ways of using your skills and expertise in more than one setting, so you aren't just swapping your labour for a pay check in your day job. This doesn't mean packing in your day job necessarily. It might mean, for example, doing some freelance work either in the same area or a completely unrelated area where you also have skills and expertise (maybe you have a hobby which means you have other skills and expertise that could be used?). Is there anything you could teach or consult on, or that you could set up as a business?

When I say 'create' new income streams, what I mean is create them *for you*. They can be old ones in the marketplace. Just make sure that you are maximizing all your skills to bring in income, and that you are actively investing in assets that will earn money for you without you having to be there (I do realize you can't physically clone yourself).

> # THE RICH USUALLY HAVE
> # SEVERAL MONEY-MAKING
> # SCHEMES GOING FOR THEM

Learn to play 'What if?'

When deciding how to earn your money and how to invest your money, you need to ask yourself a lot of questions starting with 'What if...?'

I'll start you off here:

- 'What if there is another recession?'
- 'What if this bank goes bust and I can't get my money out?'
- 'What if these shares suddenly take a turn for the worse?'
- 'What if gold prices plummet?'
- 'What if all my customers went elsewhere for a cheaper service/product?'
- 'What if I was made redundant?'
- 'What if property prices bottom out?'
- 'What if the oil runs out?'

The 'What if' game is one we can all play. All together now... 'What if...?' I call it 'looking for loopholes', only it isn't loopholes, more a sort of gotcha clause. Every time I start making some serious money, I figure someone somewhere is playing a gotcha clause whereby the unexpected happens and that particular income stream dries up rapidly. Part of the fun of being prosperous is in spotting the gotcha clause long before it happens and getting your money out and into another investment. It's also vital to consider when you are thinking about where to find extra income from. That's where having lots of hats comes in.

A good example of the dangers of putting all your eggs in one basket are the footballers who have been forced to retire while in their twenties. One minute they are earning millions and seemingly at the peak of their career and then they shatter their ankle, and their financial dreams too. They haven't trained for anything else because it never occurred to them that they might need another string to their bow.

Diversification is the name of the game – by having more than one income stream, and a nice broad spread of investments, whatever happens in the 'What if…?' scenario you will be in a much more secure position than if all your proverbial eggs are in the one basket. By asking 'What if…?' you are minimizing risks to your wealth and wealth creation.

> # DIVERSIFICATION IS THE
> # NAME OF THE GAME

Control spending impulses

The surest way to scupper your wealth creation is to go out and spend everything you earn or receive (and a bit more just for good measure). This particular addiction is very strong in me. I blame it all on giving up smoking. I have nothing to do now with my hands, so fiddling with a credit card seems to satisfy some deeply buried addictive urge. But you have to resist if you are going to turn what little you have into a bigger something. Forget notions of new cars and holidays in the sun. You are going to turn into a bit of a Scrooge for a while, hanging on to what you've got in order to prepare for the future when you will have so much more. This means you have to control your urges.

Look, I'm going to let you into a secret. Prosperity is a race, a prize, a winning line. We all set out wanting to race towards it, claim it. Some can't be bothered to even make it to the starting line because they are so weighed down with unhelpful beliefs that floor them before they start. And a whole lot of people fall by the wayside from laziness early on. And many more fail to make the grade because they get daunted by the hard work needed. And still more at this point, where you're at now, stumble because they give into temptation and spend, spend, spend like there is no tomorrow.

Well, there is a tomorrow and it comes quickly enough. And that shiny new car now looks sad and rusty, the holiday is gone with only a few snaps of people and places you can't even remember, and the new clothes are outgrown and unworn.

The simple truth is the rich know how to control their spending urges – that's why they're rich. When they need to tighten their belts they can do it.

And you need to do it too, tighten your belt that is. In fact what you need to do is not loosen it in the first place. We've talked about delayed pleasures in earlier Rules and I hope you've absorbed that one by now. Curbing those spending urges is absolutely vital and the best way to do it is to never buy anything instantly. If you see something you just have to have, wait a week. Do you still really need/want it? Chances are the urge will pass if you allow it to. Make it harder for yourself by putting time and distance between you and temptation.

> ## THE RICH KNOW HOW TO CONTROL THEIR SPENDING URGES – THAT'S WHY THEY'RE RICH

Don't answer ads that promise get-rich-quick schemes – it won't be you who gets rich quick

Last time I typed 'Opportunities to make money' into Google I got over 258,000,000 hits. That's not quite as many as 'sex'* but still a pretty good indicator of what we want. There are a lot of get-rich-quick schemes in there. Now, believe me, they do work. What? I hear you cry. Yes, indeed they do work. But not for you, not for the poor mugs who sign up. They work for the instigators, the beginners, the ones who launch such schemes.**

In the 1980s there were a lot of water purifier selling schemes about. I was invited to a couple of their meetings and went along out of interest (strictly research I promise) and was amazed at how quick people were to join in, to sign something, anything, that promised them loads of money with minimum effort. After all, what did they have to do but sell a water filter to a few friends and relations? Easy pickings they all thought. Where are all the people now who signed up, invested their savings, were promised untold riches? Funny, I can't find any either.

Maybe a few did indeed sell some and alienated their loved ones in the process. Maybe there were a few at the beginning who did make quite a bit of money. But any pyramid scheme isn't sustainable and will collapse once it reaches a certain level because there just aren't enough people on the planet to sustain the promise.

---

* 2,860,000,000 when I Googled 'sex' but 'God' is up there with 1,640,000,000 and 'work' is a staggering 6,210,000,000 so maybe there's hope for us yet.
** 137,000,000 last time I Googled 'get-rich-quick schemes'.

I like what Woody Allen says about a fool and his money – how did they get together in the first place?*

When I was a kid I remember reading about a couple of scams that set me thinking about how gullible people are. The first was a pest killer. You sent off £5 (it may have been pounds or dollars or whatever) to buy a pest killer guaranteed to kill any household pest including fleas, cockroaches, mice, etc. What you got back were two small blocks of wood with the instruction to catch and place the pest on block A and then press down block B with great force. I kid you not. And the perpetrators made a lot of money before they got caught. Might be time to try that one again. The second scam was someone offering a yard of silk during a silk crisis for a similar small fee (notice how the amount is always small enough to tempt you in) and what you got back was a yard of silk thread – they had never specified the width.

Now you might be thinking you are too clever to be taken in by such obvious hoaxes. Yes? Well, they aren't all as obvious and you might not believe the schemes that otherwise very smart people sign up to. There are no get-rich-quick schemes. Repeat after me: There are no . . .

> 'A FOOL AND HIS MONEY –
> HOW DID THEY GET TOGETHER
> IN THE FIRST PLACE?'

---

* It may not have been Woody Allen of course – he does get a lot of quotes attributed to him, especially cynical ones about money and God. Woody also said – and it was definitely him this time – that money was better than poverty if only for financial reasons.

There are no secrets

Just as there are no get-rich-quick schemes, so there are no secrets – so don't go buying any of them either. You will be offered loads. Once your attention is focused on becoming prosperous, all sorts of offers are going to come at you out of the woodwork. And they'll all offer to let you in on the secrets only the really rich know.

You'll get offered very expensive newsletters that will tell you the hidden secrets of Wall Street, how to play the Stock Exchange and win, how to invest and make a fortune, how to move your money around in offshore accounts to avoid paying taxes. And it'll cost you so little! All you've got to do is sign up for 12 monthly issues.

Guess what? The only secret being sold is the one that says there's a mug born every minute. And now you know that secret, you too can just say no. No one but you is going to make you wealthy. No one in the whole wide world. They don't know more than you. They don't have access to any more information than you do.

**NO ONE BUT YOU IS GOING
TO MAKE YOU WEALTHY.
NO ONE IN THE WHOLE
WIDE WORLD**

The secret of making money is that there are no secrets. You buy something and if you sell it for more than you paid, you've done well. And that applies to anything and everything in the financial world – stocks and shares and investments and property portfolios and ISAs and budget funds and finance management and commodity futures and FTSE and gold reserves and conch shells.

One of the earliest Rules we had to learn was that only industrious people can be prosperous. Can you see why now? You have to put in a bit of effort to learn how to do it by studying the wealthy. If you think there are shortcuts, like buying get-rich-quick schemes or buying secrets, not only are you going to be disappointed but you'll be worse off than if you hadn't invested in such nonsense. Lazy people not only don't get rich but they often end up poorer because they look for such shortcuts.

Don't just read this – do something

Time to shift some weight off that backside I'm afraid and actually do something. Reading this book is a start but it'll count for nothing unless you actually take action. You've probably thought to yourself while reading this book 'Oh I know that!' or 'That's so obvious…' OK, you know it, but have you actually done something about it? Sure, parts are obvious but does that mean you've got it sorted? For most of us there is a huge gap between what we know and what we do. There's no point just reading this, you have to act on whatever it spurs you to think would be a good idea.

Let's take it as slowly as you want. I do appreciate that changing direction is often hard; developing new character traits can be painful. Begin by changing what you watch and what you read. Begin by simply reading/watching a bit of business news. Begin by changing your awareness of what money is all about and how our money myths influence each and every interaction we have with it.

> **CHANGING DIRECTION IS OFTEN HARD; DEVELOPING NEW CHARACTER TRAITS CAN BE PAINFUL**

The way to change our mindset is to change the way we behave and the way we conduct ourselves.

- Watch how you talk, and think, about money. Do you praise its many virtues or denigrate it as something evil and negative? If you begin to talk it up you'll be surprised how quickly it materializes.

- Watch how you walk. Do you slouch and give off an air of resigned acceptance? Or are you upright and confident and looking as if you are hungry for change? (See also Rule 24.)

- Watch your overall image too. Plead poverty all the time and people will assume you are poor and act accordingly. The best thing to do is to 'act as if' you are already rich and people will adjust their perception of you and reaction to you accordingly.

Many people will fall by the wayside, despite claiming they want to be rich or richer, but they will do so not from a lack of desire. Instead it will be from a lack of motivation, a lack of doing something. Start now, right now, today, immediately.

GETTING EVEN WEALTHIER

Once you've got a bit of money behind you, the whole thing gets a bit easier. Money begets money. You won't pick up a lot of bargains at an antiques auction for £50. But there's a hell of a lot more if you've got £5000. It's that first million that is difficult – ho ho. But seriously, once you have started to move towards prosperity it isn't a good idea to sit back and start counting your loot. It'll disappear faster that way than by any other means. Instead you've got to get slicker and quicker, stay on your toes, be even busier and more focused and definitely don't take your eye off the ball.

As you start to get richer, you might need to start gathering a few advisers around you, people you can trust and, most importantly, listen to. The reason? Because as your investments and capital start to grow, you will need advice and help to make things grow even more. Obviously you can listen, but you will need to make the final decisions about what you are going to do.

Not sitting back on your laurels means you have to be on the lookout for hidden opportunities to take your prosperity further. You've got to stay abreast of current developments, play your hunches, understand the market, know what you've got and what you can spend/invest/save.

Now is the time to start stepping up how opportunistic you can be – thinking laterally, not following the herd, being creative and innovative – that sort of thing. There's no point in doing what everyone else does if you want to make some serious money...

RULE 70

Carry out a finance health check regularly

It is essential if you are going to increase your prosperity that you maintain a healthy awareness of your bank balance. You should be carrying out a finance health check on a regular basis. I think, personally, it should be weekly. Of course, you are free to do it as often as you want and if that means monthly or even longer, then that is entirely up to you but I wouldn't recommend that you leave it too long.

My observation is that the tighter a grip you have on the pulse of your financial life:

- the quicker you can react to changes

- the more information you have to make decisions

- the less chance there is for things to go drastically wrong without you noticing

- the better a focus – and thus interest – you'll have in your finances.

Sorry, but you do have to be disciplined about this. You have to have a regular time when you sit down and:

- carry out a bank reconciliation

- list your creditors and debtors

- check credit card balances against receipts

- check outstanding payments – the ones that you've authorized that haven't yet arrived in the bank

- check what future income you have and what major expenses you might have looming on the horizon

- check your standing orders

- check pensions contributions

- check investments

- check any loans

- check any overdrafts etc. (I know, I know, I have said not to have any but you are human).

If you don't do this stuff money will leak away. Forgetting a debt doesn't pay it.

You've got to be disciplined and have a routine – every Monday morning without fail. Yep, even when it's sunny outside, even on holiday, even when you're feeling a bit off-colour, even when there are more exciting things going on. Because if this doesn't excite you, then you're not going to make it I'm afraid.

Personally, I think you should know what you are earning day by day. And you should know what big outgoings you might face in the next 12 months and that does include a most often forgotten one – the tax bill. Watch that little baby like a hawk and don't ever take your eyes off that ball because it will get you every time.

> # FORGETTING A DEBT
> # DOESN'T PAY IT

Get some money mentors

When not writing books, I do have a proper job. I have several in fact, which all involve running companies. I'm no fool when it comes to knowledge. I know there are things I should know that I don't know. And there must be millions of things I don't even know I don't know. My solution is to use other people's knowledge to supplement my own deficits. I have money mentors. In fact I have mentors for all sorts of situations but we'll stick to the money ones for the moment.

Now why should you use money mentors?

- They bring a wider range of experience to the table.

- They make you present your ideas in a clear and concise format – which makes you think long and hard about what you are doing.

- They will make you justify what you are doing – this makes it much harder for you to go off like a loose cannon.

- They are on tap to provide answers, advice, as a sounding platform, a reining-in service and a 'Have you thought it through?' facility.

- They will individually keep their ear to the ground so you can benefit from their collective knowledge (a bit like a news-gathering service).

- They are independent and so will have no vested interest in what you do as competition.

- They are independent and thus will be loyal, supportive and on your team.

Many successful entrepreneurs use mentors when they start out in business. They find somebody who has been successful in starting and running their own businesses, and they ask if they would be prepared to offer guidance and advice (and sometimes contacts and more) to the new entrepreneur as they start out. The vast majority of experienced businesspeople approached will say yes – it's fun for them to pass on their expertise. They enjoy it.

Yes, but I have questions, I hear you say. Fire away.

- What sort of mentor do I need?
- Where do I find them?
- What's it going to cost me?
- Can I ignore them if I don't agree with their advice?

For a money mentor you need people who have proved their financial acumen by making a bit of money themselves – and not by inheritance or lottery winnings. You find them by looking around you. Anyone you admire who has been successful – approach them – they may well be flattered.

It shouldn't cost you more than about four decent lunches a year. You take them out to lunch. In return they give you advice, information, suggestions, restraint, support and encouragement.

And can you ignore what they say if you don't like it? Yes, of course you can. I ignored mine once. Just the once. It cost me a lot to ignore them. I publicly apologized to them and wouldn't ever ignore them again.

> **MONEY MENTORS ARE PEOPLE WHO HAVE PROVED THEIR FINANCIAL ACUMEN BY MAKING A BIT OF MONEY THEMSELVES**

RULE 72

Play your hunches

Have a hunch. Listen to your heart. Follow your intuition. Listen to your inner voice. Have gut feeling. Have an inkling. These are all saying the same thing. There are times when:

- you know something stinks
- you know when something is absolutely right
- you need to nod your head and believe in yourself.

Of course having a hunch, following a hunch and going off like a loose cannon are not all the same thing.

There is a format to this intuition lark and it is a little bit more sensible than you'd think:

- have the hunch
- do your research and see if your hunch is worth following – it usually is but best to just check first
- prepare a well-worked proposal to present to your money mentors
- present
- listen and act on their advice.

And there is no point whingeing, 'But I had this really brilliant hunch!' If you can't back up your hunch with facts and figures then it is just a stab in the dark. A hunch is a sudden flash of inspiration, a moment of sublime intuition, a clever and brilliant realization. And it can be justified with facts and figures. Just because the inspiration was a hunch doesn't mean you don't have to justify it and research it. You still need to prepare some figures and develop a plan. Having a hunch doesn't let you off being sensible and practical and realistic.

> OF COURSE HAVING A
> HUNCH, FOLLOWING A
> HUNCH AND GOING OFF
> LIKE A LOOSE CANNON ARE
> NOT ALL THE SAME THING

Lots of wealthy people got there by having that one truly brilliant moment of inspiration. But they then turned that inspiration into perspiration (sorry) and worked their guts out to make their dream come true. And I bet loads of people said to them, 'But you're so lucky'. Bah. No such thing as luck. But there is a hunch followed by hard work.

Don't sit back

There's a saying that 'Nothing wilts faster than laurels that have been rested upon'. It's very true. There is a temptation once we have made a bit of money, when an investment has worked out, or it seems to be all paying off, to sit back and relax. Yes, we can. But we don't want to. Now is the time to speed up a gear or two, put more irons in the fire. Now is the time to look around and work out our next plan of attack. Now is the time to strike, capitalize, consolidate. Now is not the time to take your eye off the ball.

We can all stir from the swamp and then settle back into the mud. But the really prosperous keep struggling until they are completely free of the slime forever. If you take a day off, the slide begins and will, inexorably, continue. And the next effort will be even harder. I know, I've been there.

So redouble your efforts. Rekindle the enthusiasm. Relight the fires of desire and let's get back to work.

> **NOW IS THE TIME TO STRIKE,**
>
> **CAPITALIZE, CONSOLIDATE**

You mustn't sit back. The wealthy don't take unscheduled days out, tea breaks, lunch breaks, holidays. They keep their nose to the grindstone, shoulder to the wheel, ear to the ground, back to the wall, finger on the pulse, iron in the fire, fire in their belly and hand on the tiller. Wow! Tall order. They work harder and enjoy greater rewards – and get told how lucky they are.

You've got to keep on doing whatever it was that made you make it. If it's a cash cow, ride that baby until it dies under you. If it was a one-off brainwave, have another. If it was sheer hard work, keep going. If you've found a successful formula, make some more. But whatever you do don't turn off the tap unless it's run dry. And even then keep it turned on just in case.

Remember, don't get clever. Don't think you know it all. Keep using those money mentors. Keep working harder than anyone around you. Keep it under your hat and keep at it.

But don't forget how you got to where you are – location, method, plan, mission. Remember the 'Don't fiddle' rule and don't change anything until you are sure it will only improve results and not make the boat sink.

Get someone to do the stuff you can't

I have money mentors because there is loads of stuff to do with business and making money that I know nothing about. There are also loads of things which have to be done which I don't know how to do. I could learn, but it isn't where my talents lie. So why go learning how to do things when there are eminently more suitable people out there who can do them? Do what you are good at and get others to do the things you can't. Simple. Pick really good people, and let them get on with the job of making you really prosperous.

Now there are ten rules to making sure you (a) get the right people and (b) keep the right people.

1 Know exactly what it is you want done and who you want to do it.

2 Be very clear about what you want them to do for you and how much you will pay and what guidelines you will give them.

3 Care about them – they are human and mustn't become a mere tool.

4 Keep them informed and motivated – inspire loyalty.

5 Tell them your long-term strategy – they too have a stake in your/their future.

6 If they muck up – and they will from time to time, we all do ('Even you, Mr Templar?' Well, maybe not me) – then correct it and move on. Forgiveness is a good thing.

7 Praise them constantly – nothing inspires more than praise (oh, yes, and money of course).

8 Set realistic targets but don't expect the impossible.

9 Set a good example – be someone they can respect and look up to (no one likes working for a jerk) – and set high standards and live up to them yourself.

10 Remember you're the boss, not their friend. Try to maintain dignity, distance and authority.

That should do it. There may be other things you will try, adapt, implement and use. All this stuff is adaptable and entirely up to you. Just make sure you treat your people well and have fun. Don't be an insensitive bossy boss – as if!

At the moment I have a wonderful accounts person. She sighs a lot as I'm always trying to find ways to ensure I'm not paying more tax than I need to – don't we all? But all I do is ask her questions. The rest I leave entirely up to her and the relationship works. Apart from the sighing that is.

> # PICK REALLY GOOD PEOPLE AND LET THEM GET ON WITH MAKING YOU REALLY PROSPEROUS

RULE 75

Know yourself – solo, duo or team player

If you are going to change direction – in this case to prosperity from wherever it is you are now – then you need to know:

- your strengths and weaknesses

- what you are good at – and bad at obviously (and this isn't the same as strengths and weaknesses).

For example, I'm good at broad strokes, big picture stuff but I'm not the greatest when it comes to detail.

Get what I'm on about? You just have to know yourself pretty well and then you will be confident in the areas you are good at, can brush up in areas you are weak, can trade on your strengths and get someone else to do all the stuff you are bad at (or haven't yet learned or researched or studied).

And then you've got to know if you are at your best working as part of a partnership, a team or going it alone. Personally I always need the steadying hand of a partner to curb some of my business excesses – an overwhelming tendency to shoot from the hip, be a bit undiplomatic at times, to rush head-long into things, to spend money wastefully on advertising and not to attend to the detail. I am, however, really bad in a team of more than two. So if a business opportunity comes up that requires teamwork I know I can turn it down or tailor it in some way, because I know if I say yes, I will make a pig's ear of it. If, however, it requires a partnership, I'm much more likely to be interested.

> # I ALWAYS NEED THE STEADYING HAND OF A PARTNER TO CURB SOME OF MY BUSINESS EXCESSES

I am also good working alone. I make decisions easily (not always the right ones but at least I don't prevaricate), I am happy in my own company for long periods and don't need to bounce ideas off anyone to make them seem real. I can travel well alone and can speak up for myself. See what I mean about knowing yourself?

You have to do this exercise if you are to forge ahead with the rest of the moneymakers. Questions to ask:

- Am I good on my own or do I need other people around me?

- Do I have a role to play in a team and feel happier in that role?

- Can I work well with just one trusted partner?

- Do I know where my strengths and weaknesses are and do I know the difference?

- Do I know what I am good and bad at?

My business partner says we work well together because we are the 'brains and brawn'. The only trouble is we both see ourselves as the brains and the other as the brawn. Oh well.

Look for the hidden asset/opportunity

You've got to be a vigilant, never-sleeping, never-taking-time-off machine. Always alert, always on the lookout for that opportunity. An old Senegalese proverb says that the opportunities that God sends do not wake up those who are asleep. Wake up! Sleep is for the lazy, the indolent, the poor. Wide awake, restless, prowling is for the hungry, the lean, the opportunity taker, the rich. All around us all of the time there are opportunities to make a fortune. All we have to do is be open to the possibilities, to the magic of such events.

There are only five things you need to take on board if you are going to be a treasure seeker:

1 **Remember that timing is crucial**. React too slowly and the opportunity is gone. Too fast and you might startle it. Markets shift, fashions change and products fade.

2 **Be serious**. There is no point in being on the ball every other day or only in the mornings. Hidden opportunities only reveal themselves when they feel they want to. I always imagine them as small shy beasts coming down to the waterhole for a drink. If you want to catch one you have to creep up really quietly, really skilfully.

3 **Be quirky**. If there are only a few hidden opportunities then you need to stand out. Quirky, unique, special, creative, unusual – name it however you will, but you have to stand out from the herd (to complete the animal analogy).

4 **Know what you're doing**. Wealth, like any other skill, needs to be learnt. To spot opportunities and to be able to take advantage of them you need to give yourself the best chance. You can't pick up a financial paper and say you are going

to understand it from Day 1. It takes time, dedication and commitment. Know your stuff and you'll see the opportunities much more clearly. There's a management technique called 'SWOT analysis' – an acronym for 'strengths, weaknesses, opportunities and threats' – keep looking at all four.

5 **Be attractive**. If you smell horrid that shy beast is going to bolt. You have to dress smartly, smell fresh, look good, be well turned out and radiate attractiveness.

> ## THE OPPORTUNITIES GOD SENDS DO NOT WAKE UP THOSE WHO ARE ASLEEP

All around us all of the time there are opportunities to make a fortune. All we have to do is be open to the possibilities, to the magic of such events.

Have you ever noticed that when you are thinking of changing cars to another make or model you immediately start noticing hundreds of that make on the roads? Were they there before? Of course. It's just that you never noticed them. But once your attention is focused like a narrow beam of intense light, it throws them into sharp focus.

Opportunities are a bit like that. Once we start noticing them they are all around us. We just need that kick-start, that beginning of the search. Just like changing cars, we change our focus.

It is essential that we wake up our opportunity detector. Once we do, opportunities will appear as if by magic all around us.

Don't try to get rich too quickly

We've already said you need to think long term. Trying to get rich quick only leads to disappointment and over-anxious hustling. And you do need to build a good base or your financial castle can topple at the first gust of wind. The longer you take to make your money, the more diverse you'll be with investments and income streams.

The quicker you make your money, the more likely it'll be a single strand and thus easy to break.

> THE LONGER YOU TAKE TO MAKE YOUR MONEY, THE MORE DIVERSE YOU'LL BE WITH INVESTMENTS AND INCOME STREAMS

Getting rich over time usually means you'll:

- build long-term income streams
- be insured against recession or sudden and negative market downturns

- have time to have a life as well – that old work/home relationship is less likely to be fractured

- be better at making money honestly and decently

- have time to make the relevant adjustments and thus not so likely to rush out and spend inappropriately

- gain the experience necessary for long-term financial security as you go along.

If you make your money too quickly there is a tendency to:

- spend it inappropriately

- not have time to learn to handle it well

- risk losing it by having your income coming from one area only.

If you really do want to earn a lot quickly you might like to take a leaf out of 79-year-old Stella Liebeck's book. She sued McDonald's because she burnt herself with spilt hot coffee and was awarded initially $2.9 million – later knocked down to a mere $640,000.

This may not have been a deliberate game plan but it did pay off – and quickly. Personally I would rather make my money slowly and enjoyably and not have to sue anyone to get it – or win the lottery, or have a close relative die, or have to marry someone inappropriate merely because they had a quid or two. Make your money slowly and you'll enjoy it more. It will last longer and you'll sleep nights.

Always ask what's in it for them

I don't want you to be paranoid generally but it is OK to be paranoid when it comes to your money. There are a lot of sharks out there looking for easy pickings from the less awake among us. Watch out.

Jeremy Paxman, the UK broadcaster, always interviews politicians with a basic underlying assumption that they are hiding something and he has to find out what and why.

Obviously we don't want to go round believing everybody is out to get us, but there is a good technique here that we can adopt to question anyone offering:

- a money-making proposition
- to 'look after' our money
- to invest in our future or schemes
- any financial advice
- to work for us
- a partnership
- products or services.

And I do mean 'offering'. If they come looking for you, rather than waiting for you to approach them for advice, you should be extremely wary.

You have to be suspicious of anyone and anything that could make inroads into your wealth. Be very wary of anybody who:

- promises to help you get rich quick, by short-cuts, using tax loopholes or dubiously legal schemes

- uses the word 'offshore'

- uses the letters MLM* or pyramid selling

- claims to be incredibly wealthy and is offering to share their secrets with you – the secret is they make their money out of people like you (see Rule 68)

- offers to increase your wealth by using the internet

- asks for money upfront to seed investment, pay for promotional material or carry out a survey.

And three things to always remember:

- If it waddles like a duck and quacks like a duck then it is a duck and don't let anyone tell you it isn't.

- If it looks too good to be true it probably is.

- Not all that glitters is gold.

> # BE SUSPICIOUS OF ANYONE
> # AND ANYTHING THAT
> # COULD MAKE INROADS
> # INTO YOUR WEALTH

Remember also to keep asking 'What's in it for this person?' Don't trust anyone. Don't give your money to anyone to look after for you. Check the small print of anything you sign. Be on your guard.

---

* Multi-level marketing.

RULE 79

Make your money work for you

An awful lot of us are guilty of wasting money by not making the best use of it – whether it's a small amount or large, long term or short term. From not cashing cheques to leaving cash in low interest accounts because you've forgotten about it or can't find the time or be bothered to move it.

Here are a few tips to get you thinking about whether you are making all your money work for you:

- Don't leave money inactive in bank accounts – move it around to high interest accounts, even if it's only for a few days. Electronic banking means money can be easily and simply switched from one account to another – even for very short periods.

- Never be satisfied with the interest rate you are getting – there's always a better one out there. Keep actively looking.

- Shop around for all services you pay for. There are always cheaper options. Don't just pay for a name, pay for what you are getting.

- Don't leave property empty – it may be increasing in value but you are missing valuable rental income.

- If you invest in anything that is appreciating in value, could it also be useful? Would a classic car you can drive be more useful to you as opposed to a painting you can only look at (although that could be regarded as useful in the sense it might be relaxing or therapeutic but let's not go there).

- Explore all options. Don't be content ever with what you are doing but always be on the lookout for ways to improve, enhance, perk up, progress and advance. This does not mean fiddling of course.

- Crack on. Don't put anything off for tomorrow. Do it today. Do it now. If you take four months to bank a cheque then that's four months' interest you've lost.

- Always remember idle money is wasted money – use it or lose it.

NEVER BE SATISFIED WITH
THE INTEREST RATE YOU
ARE GETTING

RULE 80

Know when to let go of investments

I have my own little calculation which I am happy to pass on to you. I learned it from an internet site a while back and it has stood me in good stead. Basically for an investment to work for me means I am generally looking for a return that will double my money in five years. In a recession I might extend that to, maybe, seven years – of course the higher/faster the return, the higher the risk.

The calculation I use is to divide the interest rate into 72 to find out how long it will take me to double my money. For example, if the interest rate on a particular investment is 6 per cent, then it will take me 12 years ($72 \div 6 = 12$) to double my money. Too long for me. So I would be looking for an interest rate (known as a 'return') of around 14.4 per cent (I know, I know, you'd be lucky at the moment but this is only an example). This works for any amount of money incidentally.

So, if you want to know what interest rate to look for divide 72 by the number of years you are prepared to wait. $72 \div 5 = 14.4$ per cent. Gosh, something useful for you there and I did all the work for you.

For me, therefore, any investment that looks like it won't double my money in five years I pass on or, if it makes financial sense to get out (i.e. no penalty for doing so), I will let go of. I have my criteria, you need yours.

Perhaps you need to let go when:

- you feel in your waters that something is not right

- the market has taken a downturn

- you read something that makes you curious or suspicious of a particular investment

- you need the money for something better, hotter

- the investment hasn't been doing well for a while and is sluggish

- you've achieved your maximum profit and it's time to get out

- you've lost interest in a particular investment and simply can't be bothered any more

- you have changed emotionally or ideologically and need to move on – perhaps you only invested green and now want mainstream or vice versa

- the investment isn't fashionable any more – old hat can be costly if the return isn't there

- you need to spread your portfolio around to minimize losses in a recession or down market

- you bought blind and now have more information – and can see your fingers getting burnt

- throwing good money after bad will just aggravate the situation – cut your losses and get out (see Rule 81).

> ## PERHAPS YOU ONLY INVESTED GREEN AND NOW WANT MAINSTREAM OR VICE VERSA

Know your own style

We all have a tendency to buy on tips from other people, buy on a whim, buy glamorous, invest too much in one thing, ride a winner to death and, most fatally of all, fail to quit a loser. This is the one habit we must really learn to let go of.

There are different approaches to investing of course, and you need to recognize your own style. Otherwise you can't learn to curb your worst tendencies. So I'm going to give you a few examples, and I want you to be brutally honest about recognizing which one is you.

Are you competitive? If so, you're likely to have plenty of enthusiasm and get in early. You've probably taken the trouble to learn about your investments. However, you may be over-confident and optimistic, and prone to chase a losing streak.

Of course you may be more solid – careful, secure and long-termist. A wise approach, but again still prone to chase a bad luck run.

Then there are the investors who aren't really sure they want to be there. If you're this type, you probably use an adviser, and take a long time (maybe too long) to decide to invest. You're good at letting go of losers. The chief downside is that while you probably won't sustain huge losses, you may not make the big bucks others do.

Some investors don't prepare themselves well. They invest too little, too late, they are likely to put too many eggs in one basket (maybe following a tip) and take too long to let go when things go downhill.

The trouble is that emotions and personality can get in the way of successful investing. Characteristics such as optimism, over-cautiousness, competitiveness, impatience, fear, desperation and all the rest can easily sway you. But this is your retirement, your house, your luxury holiday, your kids' inheritance you're gambling with, and you need to make sure that you do it in a clinical, calculated, risk-assessed fashion.

It is imperative that you know what type of investor you are – and when to quit riding a losing streak. Nothing clouds your judgement more than throwing good money after bad. You have to learn to cut your losses and walk away. And yes, I do know how hard that can be.

> # EMOTIONS AND PERSONALITY CAN GET IN THE WAY OF SUCCESSFUL INVESTING

RULE 82

Know why you should be able to read a balance sheet – and how

If you are going to run a company or invest in companies, you need to be able to read a balance sheet. This is different to knowing what profit or loss a company has made (i.e. reading a profit and loss account). Why? Because a profit and loss account only shows you half the picture.

For instance, Company X might have a turnover of 1 million and expenses of 500,000, thus it has made a profit of 500,000 and must be doing really well, n'est-ce pas? No, actually. Because what you can't see from this simple profit and loss account is that it owes the bank 2 million, the 1 million in turnover is very dodgy and there is a 4 million tax bill hanging over its head from previous years' accounts, a franchise expiring, a tax loophole about to close and a powerful competitor about to start up. Invest in Company X? I don't think so. It's bankrupt and fraudulently trading and not worth a pig's ear. Stay away. So you need to see a balance sheet. Without fail. And because of what it is not telling you.

A balance sheet has to balance. That's why it's called a balance sheet.* The basic formula you need to know is assets minus liabilities = equity or A − B = C. Into even simpler terms: what you own less what you owe equals what you are worth. This applies to yourself, companies you work for/own and companies you intend investing in. Let's have a closer look.

---

* The actual balance is equity + liabilities = assets, thus balancing. You get assets on one side and liabilities and equity on the other.

- **What you own – your assets**. This includes current assets, including cash and anything that can be realized (i.e. turned into cash) within say a three-month period (this might include cast-iron debtors, money in transit etc.); stock (stuff ready to be sold and raw materials that have value and can be made into products); any property you or the company may own; equipment and goodwill.

- **What you owe – your liabilities**. This includes your creditors, long-term loans and bank loans. Basically what you would have to find in cash if everyone called in what you owed them.

- **What you are worth – your equity**. This is A minus B. It tells us what you or your company is really worth. There is a formula that says that you take your current assets and divide it by your liabilities and if the answer is bigger than 1.5 you're doing OK. Obviously you need to adjust this for different industries and businesses but it serves as a basic indicator. I also take the equity and divide it by the assets as a percentage. And if the answer is higher than 50, I feel confident. For instance, equity 35 million ÷ by assets (capital employed) of 70 million as a percentage = 35,000,000 ÷ 70,000,000% = 50 which is fine. But assets of 120 million and equity of 35 million is not so hot – around 29.

So if you just hear about a company that has made a profit of 1 million and are offered the chance to invest, don't be impressed by that single figure. Ask to see the balance sheet. Read it thoroughly. In fact, don't just read the balance sheet, important as it is – there are other things you need to know, such as a company's financial statements in total. The more information you can get (and should get), the more solid your decision will be.

> ## A BALANCE SHEET
> ## HAS TO BALANCE

Be one step ahead of your tax collector

You must never ever try to evade paying your taxes. If you do you will go to prison – and quite rightly so. No, I am not on the side of the tax collector. There's a difference here between evade (criminal) and avoid (sensible). There is a line between making sure you aren't giving money unnecessarily to the tax collector – avoiding – and deliberately evading tax illegitimately. Cross that line at your peril. But there should be no need to do so. There are many good people out there who will give you all the advice you need.

The more money you have, the greater the need to avoid tax – I stress this is not the same thing at all as evading – and the more expensive it becomes to do so. Obviously there is a tipping point whereby you are obliged to hand over your tax affairs to experts – who naturally cost an arm and leg – so you can avoid paying the tax collectors the other arm and leg you have left.

> **THERE ARE MANY GOOD PEOPLE OUT THERE WHO WILL GIVE YOU ALL THE ADVICE YOU NEED**

As you move up the prosperity ladder the tax issues get more complex. And there are all sorts of options. But remember the tax collectors are closing loopholes, changing laws, cutting off avenues as fast as you and your expensive experts can devise ways of avoiding tax. It's like a chess game only much more exciting and expensive.

I am not going to give you any specific advice because it changes too quickly and I don't want to get sued, but areas worth bearing in mind are:

- Consider establishing a limited company – it can attract less tax and give you all sorts of options not available to the 'self-employed'. I'm assuming you are making some money – if you aren't, there is obviously no tax to save as there is no tax to pay. Bear in mind also that anyone can get your company records from Companies House so if you are bigging yourself up you can get caught out.

- Always make sure you make full use of your allowances – use them or lose them.

- Always consider if something is tax deductible before you buy it.

- Become a resident in a tax haven – but be quick as they are being shut down fast.

- Invest heavily in your own pension fund – it grows tax free, or as about tax free as you can get these days.

- Become a tax nomad and wander the world not paying tax anywhere – watch out as a UK tax liability will arise when either income or a capital gain is remitted into the UK and there are circumstances when you can be based abroad but still pay tax (it depends on residency, ordinarily residency and domicile).

And, of course, make sure you are well up on investments that you don't have to pay tax on – get good advice and be willing to pay for good advice.

RULE 84

Learn how to make your assets work for you

First off, do you know what assets you have? This means both long-term assets (fixed assets) and short-term assets (current assets). The fixed assets are the ones it would take you a while to turn into cash and the current assets are the ones easily converted into readies. Have you listed them? If not, do so now. I'll wait.

Back already? Got your list? I hope it has some of the following on it:

- property
- land
- motor vehicles
- pension funds
- cash
- goodwill
- works of art, antiques etc.
- investments
- money owed
- furniture and other possessions
- patents
- stocks and bonds
- intellectual properties.

If you have a business it may also include things like:

- stock
- work in progress
- raw materials
- plant and machinery
- equipment
- trade marks
- mailing lists.

Once you start writing them down as a list you begin to see endless possibilities for using assets to make more money. Basically the advice is:

- Don't let an asset sit idle – if you own property, rent it out. And I don't just mean buy-to-let. Some enterprising people have rented garages or small bits of land they don't use in areas where there isn't enough parking for commuters and so on. Think laterally and don't discount anything!

- No asset is beautiful unless it is working for you – it has to be accumulating, increasing in value, to be worth keeping.

- Never leave cash sitting around – it tends to get bored and wander off. Make it work.

> ## YOU BEGIN TO SEE ENDLESS POSSIBILITIES FOR USING ASSETS TO MAKE MORE MONEY

Don't ever believe you're only worth what you are being paid

Those who believe they are only worth what an employer pays them are almost always selling themselves short. Big companies depend on people not questioning their worth. Don't let them get away with it.

There are several points here. Firstly, it's a fact that if you work for an employer, those who change their jobs fairly frequently tend to get pay rises each time and therefore end up earning more than those who stay with the same company (maybe for very good reasons, like being happy). If you are staying put you have to learn to ask for more and demonstrate how you are adding value to an organization to justify being paid more.

Secondly, no company is ever going to pay more for anything than they really have to. You need to be proactive and ask for more, and show you are worth more. It requires you to take action, however. Don't wait to be recognized. If you are free-lance the same applies – nobody will suddenly offer to pay you more for your work – you need to be proactive and show you are worth more.

Thirdly, if you think you are always worth more, it makes you restless, ambitious, keen to get on. If you accept what is offered and never question it, then it makes you complacent and you'll get taken for granted.

Now this is not a book about how to get a pay rise but here are a few tips.

- Be very clear about what you think you are worth – and why. If you have worked harder, achieved more, produced more, got better results, then you are entitled to say so and ask for recompense.

- Don't bargain just for money – always take into account cars, pensions, holiday entitlements, responsibility, working environment and space, staffing, whatever it is you want.

- If you do get turned down, always find out why and what it is you could do to get what you ask for.

- Return after putting right whatever was wrong in the previous point.

- Never compare yourself with anyone else – you are unique and there is no comparison.

Getting more money – or anything else – is a matter of negotiating. Those who are good negotiators get more. It's as simple as that. Brush up on your negotiating skills (see Rule 34). And don't moan if you don't get what you want. Work harder and go back again.

> **IF YOU THINK YOU ARE
> ALWAYS WORTH MORE
> IT MAKES YOU RESTLESS,
> AMBITIOUS, KEEN TO GET ON**

RULE 86

Don't follow the same route as everyone else

Obviously you can follow whatever route you want, but you might end up in the same place as a lot of other people. If that is a good place, you'll have to share a lot. And if it's a bad place, why be there at all?

Being creative is a brilliant way to make money. Look at all the best moneymakers and one of the things they share is the ability to be one step ahead, to think creatively (out of the box if you like), to come up with schemes and ideas that other people haven't thought of. This doesn't mean you have to be reckless or a gambler. It just means thinking differently from other people. But that's the problem most people have. Following the herd is terribly comforting. If it all goes wrong, being in a herd gives a collective feeling of shared grief and the opposite of shared blame. Be a loner and going wrong is a tough cookie to swallow.

And the converse is true. If it all goes well and you are in a herd you can celebrate together – shared joy. A bit like being at a football match. It's a good feeling.

BEING CREATIVE

IS A BRILLIANT WAY

TO MAKE MONEY

It takes a person of real courage, confidence and maturity – not to mention creativity and drive – to stand up and go your own way. You've got to be pretty confident to turn your back on shared joy and shared grief. In the great stock market crash of October 1987 an awful lot of people lost an awful lot of money. Two who didn't, and got out of shares and into cash in August, were the billionaires Kerry Packer and Jimmy Goldsmith. And remember that the closer you get to becoming a winner, the less risk you want. And the nearer to losing you get, the more you are inclined to gamble.

I saw a website the other day – an investment broker's one – which claimed to show the five most popular stocks and the reasons why you should sell them now no matter what your friends, neighbours or family say. These stocks have been so high for so long that they must crash soon. Sell now and get out ahead of the crowd. I was thinking that real money-makers wouldn't have been there anyway but would have been out there investing in something none of us had even thought of.

Lots of people invested in ostrich farms. Where are they now? Lots of people invested in worm farms. You bought eggs and turned them into worms and the big worm farm would buy them back. Loved that one. Yeah, right. Of course they'll buy all your worms back off you.

One of my sons invested £10 to start his own giant snail business. He bought two giant snails to breed with (or should that be from?). He fed and looked after them for about six months when I had to break it to him they were snails out of someone's garden he'd bought. He wasn't alone. Loads of kids at his school were sold the same dream. And the same snails.

STAYING
WEALTHY

Now you've got wealth, you don't want to let it go, so the next section is how to hang on to it once you've got it. Assuming you now know to avoid the giant snail scams and the ostrich farms. How to preserve, protect, enjoy and maintain it. After all, when you've finally got it, you don't want to waste it, squander it, throw it away or give it to me. Actually the last one isn't true. You can if you really want to.

There are endless websites all offering to look after your money for you. Ignore them all. They usually say something like: 'Start your own wealth freedom journey today – no time to lose!' All you have to do is sign up for a newsletter and buy a 'get-rich-quick' book right away. They promise to make you a millionaire within three to five years.

Perhaps you should ask for a refund on this book because I promise you nothing beyond hard work, dedication, focus, creativity, standing out from the crowd, forward planning and the honest sweat of your brow. Gosh. No promises there at all.

Shop for quality

My lovely wife taught me this one – credit where it is due. When we met I was a great one for finding a bargain – two chickens for the price of one at the supermarket, that sort of thing. She, on the other hand, bought less (I never did do anything with that other chicken) but bought quality. So I would cook a thin and sick-looking chicken and drink it with cheap white plonk and she would provide lobster and champagne. You can see why I fell for her.

I bought five cheap T-shirts in a pack and she bought an immaculate one of much better quality. Now her stuff:

- lasted longer

- washed better

- looked better with age

- kept its colour better

- kept its shape better

- said more about her in a positive way

- took less maintenance (I drove a cheap car that was always breaking down and I missed meetings etc. whereas she drove a better car and always arrived looking calm and immaculate).

She taught me that the money I was spending, although less, was being wasted because I had to replace stuff much more often. I was throwing money away and looking cheap at that.

Shopping for quality rather than price was a hard lesson to learn. I had to discard all those money myths from my childhood:

- Don't spend more than you need to.

- No one needs to look that expensive.

- It is somehow wrong to spend money on yourself.

- It is somehow better to get a bargain than to buy quality.

Shopping for quality says masses about the way you live, the way you conduct yourself and your business. It says quality to others who will adjust the way they treat you. It also saves you money in the long run – cheap can often be a false economy.

> SHOPPING FOR QUALITY SAYS MASSES ABOUT THE WAY YOU LIVE, THE WAY YOU CONDUCT YOURSELF AND YOUR BUSINESS

Check the small print

I could write you a contract promising you a cast-iron, no get-out clauses, guaranteed, money back without quibbles, cross my heart and hope to die in a cellarful of rats, sort of thing that would stand up in a court of law and withstand any scrutiny you cared to put it under. What am I selling? It doesn't matter. Small print can cost you dear. Check it carefully.

I love the sort of small print classics, such as taking shoes back that don't fit only to be told they can't be refunded if they have left the store. Or the small print on medications that say they can make you sick and you can't sue. Or the small print on computer software that says you are bound by the agreement if you break the seal on the packaging – and the software can't be tested until it has been run and you can't run it until you've installed it and you can't do that until you've broken open the packaging. Agh!

> SMALL PRINT CAN COST YOU
> DEAR. CHECK IT CAREFULLY

There's a wonderful story of someone who sold their soul to the devil. The devil wanted five years off their life and the person reckoned it was worth it. Oh no! He didn't check the small print. The devil took five years off his life all right – the *first* five years. Agh! Can you imagine what missing the first five years would do to you? And you thought credit card companies were bad?

What do I mean by 'checking the small print'? What do you actually have to do? Three basic things:

- Obviously check that it covers you for what you want.

- Check there are no hidden clauses that will twist the basic meaning of the contract.

- Check for penalty clauses – ones that penalize you for late or non-payment of anything.

It's a bit like checking the small print on food packaging. If you don't like what's in it, don't buy it. Move on up the aisle and buy organic, green, fresh, unpasteurized, whatever. If there is small print, the hairs on the back of your neck should be rising. There is only one reason for it to be there – to trip you up. Move on.

Don't spend it before you've got it

Gosh, this is a hard one for me. I have to admit I find this one of the most difficult to take on board.

How am I to learn this one? Any tips?

I know I should:

- budget for today and only for today – if I don't have it, I don't spend it

- ignore what I think or know is coming in, in the future

- put loads aside for tax – no, even more than that

- have no loans, overdrafts, no borrowings of any sort so I won't be tempted to use future income to pay off debts run up today – or the reverse, run up debts today knowing that income from the future can be used to pay them off (very naughty).

The downside of spending future income is:

- the income may not materialize or be less than you thought (counting chickens that never hatch...)

- the bubble has to burst somewhere and if you are always spending in advance you will get caught out one day

- it encourages sloppy financial planning

- whatever you bought will have long lost its appeal or wear out, get broken or even completely forgotten

- you lose touch with reality – the future isn't real until it becomes today – and as such you can overspend only too easily.

I guess I need a four-point plan:

1 Question whether I need a particular thing today or could wait until later to buy it – a useful ploy as once the 'blood lust' has worn off the appeal often wears off too.

2 Question whether it is worth it. Obviously, if buying today against tomorrow's income, I will incur interest – so is it worth the extra?

3 Question the risk factor. If I commit myself today, what if my circumstances change and I need that future income for other purposes?

4 Question that if I spend today I might not have income for a really exciting spend that might come up – better to keep it just in case.

Follow this plan with me and it should reduce our credit card balances considerably.

THE FUTURE ISN'T REAL
UNTIL IT BECOMES TODAY

Put something aside for your old age – no, more than that!

When you realize you are cracking along fast in the outside lane of the age motorway and can see less road ahead than there used to be, you should be keen to make sure that if you do stop earning you will still be able to afford the level of style, luxury and comfort you now enjoy or want to enjoy.

There are some really good reasons why you should put aside money for your old age:

- You can't rely on the state any more.

- If you don't save for yourself, then you may have to rely on the kindness of strangers – or family, which might be worse.

- If you have no old age plan, you may lose control of your level of comfort, style and luxury.

- If you have no plan, you will lose control of your financial freedom.

- You may lose control of bodily functions and will need money to take care of medical bills.

- As you age you do slow up, and working as hard as you are now will be impossible.

- You also don't want to have to always work hard (though you may choose to) – for most of us there is a time for sitting in the sunshine and if it isn't when you're old, then when is it?

So why haven't we put something aside already? Well, when we are young it's hard to envisage a time when we won't be. So we don't need to prepare for it. Also, we are too busy having a good time to think about such things. Also, we are too busy looking after other members of our family to have much time to think about ourselves. Also, we are mortgaged up to the hilt and work is hard enough. Also, we haven't entered our earning boom period of our fifties so don't have lump sums to salt away. Also, also, also.

So, if we are going to put something aside, perhaps we need a few guidelines:

- It's never too late to start, but the earlier you do it, the less it will hurt. Prioritize spending – list what you are going to spend on and see if 'the future' is there. If it isn't, put it there and make it top of the list ahead of that new boat or trip to Paris.

- If you haven't saved much by your fifties put in a lump sum to seed your retirement plan.*

- Get your finances in order and curb waste – spend it instead on your plan.

- If you don't have a pension, make sure you have things that will fund your retirement/later years (property to sell? shares to cash in?) and that they will be sufficient.

- Always think high interest and move money around to get the best out of it.

Trade down property as you get older and your needs get smaller – once the kids have all left home you don't need so much space, so downsize and invest the profits.

> # THE EARLIER YOU DO IT,
> # THE LESS IT WILL HURT

---

* God, don't ever 'retire', you'll drop down dead immediately you do that.

Put something aside for emergencies/rainy days – the contingency fund

As well as saving for your old age you'll always need to have a contingency fund. I can't give you a definitive list of emergencies but here's a few to get you thinking. Don't have nightmares now:

- accidents – motoring, industrial, work-related

- illnesses

- sudden legal problems – like being sued or arrested wrongly

- land disputes – very expensive indeed

- problems with children – don't start me off, there are too many to list here including drugs, unwanted pregnancies, trouble with police, motoring, illnesses, travel problems (it's expensive to get them back from Thailand when they run out of money and/or enthusiasm)

- acts of God – floods, earthquakes, tsunami, droughts, subsidence, forest fire, pestilence (whatever that is)

- sudden unemployment

- sudden liquidation of your company

- recession.

So how much to put aside and where do we put it? Well, the wise move is to put aside enough to keep you going in the same style as you live now for three to six months without having to even think about money for that period. Roughly half your annual income if you like. Obviously if you get completely wiped out in a tsunami or forest fire you'll be insured so can collect, but you will need something to tide you over. Medical bills can also be covered by insurance.

So where to keep it? Most people keep it as a savings account – high interest of course, but instant access. Personally I've noticed the shrewd rich ones keep a safety deposit box with cash for emergencies as well. Always handy in desperate times.

You only have to look at humanitarian disasters to realize how quickly money runs out and how conventional sources become desperately difficult to access. Surviving the storms of Louisiana was bad enough for most people but it was a great leveller because no one could access the banks because they too were under 10 feet of water. And money quickly becomes a useless currency – food and water become the priorities then (and guns I believe, but I don't want to go there).

You might choose to take out sizeable insurance policies to help alleviate the problems sudden emergencies can cause... Alternatively you might prefer to squirrel away an emergency fund in a highly liquid account (easy quick access), such as a savings account or money market account (which pays higher interest rates). But, as usual, take detailed advice from a proper financial expert – not me.

> # THE SHREWD RICH ONES KEEP A SAFETY DEPOSIT BOX WITH CASH FOR EMERGENCIES

You paid what for it? How to shop around

I know I said shop for quality, and I do really believe that, but I don't believe in throwing your money away on expensive stuff that could be bought just as cheaply from another source. For instance, a dear friend was recently buying a very expensive car, a wonderful car. I was most jealous. I was so jealous I broke all my own rules and asked him what he was paying for it. I couldn't believe my ears. 'You're paying what for it?!'

He said he could afford it – as indeed he most certainly can. But it was the principle of the thing. 'You can get it a lot cheaper here, here or here,' I suggested. 'Yes,' he replied, 'but then I would have to get up off my arse and do something instead of just reaching for the phone.'

I offered to buy it for him at the cheaper location and then sell it on to him and split the difference. But he was having none of it. He explained he had earned his money so he could stay on the sofa and lift a phone and have the world brought to him, delivered with the minimum of effort. That was what he thought great wealth was all about.

Now, unlike my friend, the sensible rich don't just throw money away because they can. Instead they:

- always get at least three quotes for work being done and don't just accept the first quote they get

- shop around to make sure they aren't wasting their money

- are cautious about spending if they have had to work hard for their money. They aren't miserly, just cautious and selective and discriminating.

There is an old Russian saying that spending is quick but earning long. That's true. We can offload the work of years in a few moments. We have to be prudent when it comes to spending. Not to deny ourselves anything – God forbid I should recommend that. But instead just be a bit cautious and don't go throwing money away needlessly.

I think wise spending is something we should be teaching our kids from a very early age. They are all too often persuaded by advertising that if something is brightly coloured, noisy, messy or in some way repugnant to parents, it must be a good thing. And they rush home and strip off all those wrappings and disappointment sets in so very quickly. Teach 'em young.

As for you, time to discover for yourself the joy of getting value for money in everything you buy (if you haven't already). The internet makes it all terribly easy to compare prices and shop around and make sure you aren't paying more than you have to for anything. Use it.

> # JUST BE A BIT CAUTIOUS AND DON'T GO THROWING MONEY AWAY NEEDLESSLY

Never borrow money from friends or family (but you can allow them to invest)

I think we might need to have a quick recap of what friends and family are there for – and what you are there for, for them as well. Friends are for:

- caring

- loving

- supporting

- nurturing

- helping

- advising – and getting advice from

- comforting

- having fun with

- sharing.

Nowhere in that lot does it mention:

- borrowing from

- stealing from

- conning.

Put simply, it is very bad manners to borrow from friends and family. It sets up too many issues and agendas. It causes resentments and recriminations and suspicions. It jeopardizes relationships that are important. Don't do it.

Besides which, friends and family aren't proper sources of loans because they aren't licensed for it. I'm not talking here of the odd fiver to get a round of drinks in but significantly large amounts – how much that is will depend on your circumstances...You do need to be licensed to be a credit broker (no seriously) and if you borrow from friends (or conversely lend to the same) you have no legal recourse if it all goes wrong – and it will, as sure as eggs is eggs.

I know technically you could get proper agreements drawn up and all that but even then, and even if they are charging you the proper interest rates, it's dangerous. If you fail to pay them back – due to circumstances beyond your control – you risk losing their friendship, which of course would mean much more to you than the loan would in the first place.

The only exception to this is if family and friends want to invest in say a business you are starting, and they fully understand that, like any investment, they may not see a return and all the usual risks apply. (See Rule 97 for more on this.) What you can't afford is for it to cause a rift if things don't work out. Family and friends are too important for that.

> # IT IS VERY BAD MANNERS
> # TO BORROW FROM FRIENDS
> # AND FAMILY

Don't surrender equity

This is a Rule for anybody who runs a company, or who is a freelance and is thinking of setting themselves up as a sole trader business. Essentially the point is not to give away bits of you or your company.

The aim of the exercise is to preserve wealth so don't surrender equity (shares or a stake in your company) or you'll be paying someone a share of your hard work, time and energy. Better to give them money, even if it is with interest, rather than a share of you.

In a later Rule on spending your money I'll tell you to ask for equity, but that's different – that's you as a lender of money. The shoe is on the other bank account then, so different rules apply.

There is a misconception that having total control of one's business is a bad thing and many business advisers will advocate giving away equity as a good thing. But I have noticed that the really successful wealthy don't do this. They hang on to every bit they've got. They may borrow and take out loans and run up overdrafts but they don't give away equity.

Advisers will suggest steering clear of a bank loan because the bank can close down your business so quickly. A business angel will lend money instead, but they will demand equity.

If you do have to surrender equity then make sure you swap it for:

- business skills and acumen

- hands-on directorships

- a freedom-from-hassle agreement so you can run the business the way you want

- a realistic percentage so you don't give away too much

- a buy-back clause so you can buy back the equity for cash at a later stage when you are cash rich.

I run a company and have some shareholders but the shares they hold don't give them voting rights. So, although they do get some equity, they don't get control, and in fact the shares were given as a reward for advice rather than money I borrowed.

Only take money into your business from people who have experience of your business and understand its ebbs and flows and industry-related problems – and remember, never give voting shares away to anyone.

NEVER GIVE VOTING SHARES
AWAY TO ANYONE

Know when to stop

What? I can hear a gasp of surprise. Know when to stop?! Didn't you say earlier that you shouldn't rest on your laurels or they will wilt? Yes I did, but that was when you were starting to get results, not when you'd done really well and were wealthier than you thought you ever would be. Look, there has to come a time when enough is enough. There has to come a time when you want to:

- spend more time with your family

- enjoy your life

- have fun

- go travelling

- get the work/life balance tipped a bit in favour of the life

- use your time to pass on what you have learned to others.

> ## THERE HAS TO COME A TIME
> ## WHEN ENOUGH IS ENOUGH

Of course you might be able to do all of these without giving up the gaining wealth ideal. But it is the focus that stops perhaps. Being driven to gain prosperity is a good thing. But once gained, you should return to the fold so to speak. I am always impressed by people like Bill Gates, who decided to retire from his work to run his charitable foundation. In his case he probably didn't need and couldn't spend or count any more money than he already had/has and it's probably accumulating faster each day than he can count. He's probably living on the interest on the interest on the interest on the interest...

And I see Warren Buffet is doing the same – and actually contributing to Bill's foundation.* I know these boys are playing around with sums well into the billions but their hearts are in the right place. These sorts of people are where this rule comes from. Others doing the same include Thomas Monaghan, the Domino's Pizza founder, who is reputed to have given away over a billion dollars and founded Ave Maria University.

You're thinking that you aren't anywhere in the same league. No, but you can still have an end game strategy whereby you build an 'enough is enough' clause into your plan. Otherwise where do you stop? How much is enough? Where do you draw the line? There is an Arab saying: 'If you have much, give of your wealth; if you have little, give of your heart.' So when you get a lot, give some of it away – we'll speak more of this in a moment.

I'm not going to browbeat you about giving to charity but I am suggesting that knowing when you've got enough money is important. I know there is an expression that you can't have too much of a good thing but focusing on prosperity is only one part of a rich and varied life and you can be too dedicated.

---

* Sorry, it is actually called the Bill and Melinda Gates Foundation – BMGF – sounds like something from a story by Roald Dahl.

SHARING
YOUR WEALTH

Once you've worked hard to earn it, it does seem a bit unfair to share it. But if you don't you run the risk of your hardworking outstretched hand turning into an arthritic grasping claw. Money can be earned, grown, guarded, fought over, used well, used badly, won, lost, buried, invested, given away, bought back, exchanged and divided up. But the nicest thing to do with it is surely to share it.

I'm not talking do-gooding here. I'm talking sharing because sharing is a kind thing to do. It won't buy you a ticket into heaven but it will help others. I know you've worked hard, grafted, and burnt the midnight oil to get to where you are today and why should you give money away to those who are lazy or less focused or indulgent or plain liberty-takers? Yep, good point. But I'm talking here about the less well off, the unfortunate, the weak, the needy and the deserving.

Wealth is a bit like a beautiful painting. Sure you can hang it in your study and only you get to look at it. But you can also share it and let others look as well. Ah, but you'll say wealth decreases if we share it. Does it? Does it really? I doubt it somehow. I think for every penny you give away – or share with someone less able to gain prosperity – you double its value. Maybe not in hard cash but in other ways.

As I say, I don't want to browbeat you. It's just I've noticed that the really successful, happy rich people do feel at ease sharing their wealth and that is a lesson for all of us.

Use your wealth wisely

I read of a nice couple the other day – both rock musicians – who had bought a big house in the countryside in Oxfordshire (or some other Home County) with nine acres and were settling down to raise kids and I thought what a good investment as it provides:

- a stable place to bring up kids

- a sound investment in the long term

- a nice place to live in the sense of peace and quiet with no city pollution

- a friendly place for the children to grow up with neighbours looking out for them

- a sound investment in history and heritage.

On the other hand, I read in the same paper of a fashion model who was in the news a lot because of her drug habit. An expensive habit I have no doubt. I guess you can see where my interests lie from these two snippets gleaned from the newspapers. One is a sound and wise investment and the other is just self-indulgent trouble that lends nothing to the wisdom of wealth.

I'm not a party pooper but I have noticed that those who handle their wealth sensibly and share it and are generous with their time and money get back a whole lot more than those who squander, misuse, indulge and generally behave as if their wealth gives them a licence to show off. Enough moralizing and preaching. I did promise not to. But these are genuine observations and I'm sure you've made similar observations yourself. Those who abuse their wealth don't tend to stay wealthy for long. Here are a few questions regarding our wealth and how wisely we might handle it:

- Why did we get wealthy in the first place?

- What is the best use of wealth?

- What are our long-term goals and expectations for our wealth?

- What do we think our wealth will bring us?

- What could we do with our wealth that would be beneficial to others?

- What sort of world do we want?

- How do we and our wealth wish to be seen?

- What will they say about us after we've gone?

- What legacy will we leave behind?

> # THOSE WHO ABUSE THEIR WEALTH DON'T TEND TO STAY WEALTHY FOR LONG

I personally think the best use of wealth is to teach children how to earn it, invest it, save it and spend it wisely. As we all get more and more affluent, there is a real need to introduce some element of monetary discussion into the curriculum. Children need to learn about tax, insurance and spending and all the stuff we never got taught and have had to learn the hard way as we went along. Mind you, I would also make sure every child could read and write before they left school and could drive a car.

Never lend money to friends or family unless you are prepared to write it off

Can you share your wealth with family and friends? Yes, but if you want to retain your sanity I would strongly suggest you don't lend anyone any money unless, mentally, you are prepared to write it off. That way when they don't repay you – and I bet they won't – you'll feel just fine about it. If you expect them to repay you and they don't, imagine how hurt and let down you are going to feel.

I know. I have sons. But my money is for them as much as it is for me, so we play this game of them asking for a loan and me giving it to them. Sometimes they pay it back and I am pleasantly surprised but sometimes they don't and I write it off and that's fine too. (I really hope they don't read this or I'll be cornered like a rat in my own home.)

I value them and their relationship with me and I wouldn't want to fall out with them over something as squalid as money when there are so many better things to fall out with them over anyway.

If you do lend money to friends and don't get it back, you lose more than just the money – you lose the friendship as well. They feel embarrassed because they aren't repaying you and thus don't come round to see you. You feel grieved and don't invite them because of it. Result: end of friendship.

Write it off though and you'll still be happy to see them and they'll quickly forget the embarrassment and regard you as one of a kind.

Of course you don't have to do either. You can just say no (see Rule 100). Or you could just give them money (see Rule 101).

I've been reading an advice blog on the web about a young man who lent his room-mate at college $350 – not a huge amount – but the repayment never materialized. He had asked various friends first if they had ever lent his room-mate money and they said he had paid them back. Now he has of course fallen out big time with his room-mate – despite offering him the option of repayment terms at $50 a month. Worse still, he has fallen out with all his other friends because they 'approved' the loan in his eyes.

The advice was to take the friend to court but I figure he won't see the money anyway and will cop a lot of legal expense into the bargain. Better to chalk it up to experience and walk away whistling. I know, for him, it is a lot of money but any decent education doesn't come cheap. The discussion did go on into his rights to 'seize' his room-mate's possessions etc. I still say walk away whistling and don't ever do it again.

> ## CHALK IT UP TO EXPERIENCE AND WALK AWAY WHISTLING

RULE 98

Don't lend, take equities

If you are asked for a loan by somebody for a specific project such as starting a company or expanding one, there are a variety of answers including:

- no

- yes

- yes but

- yes on the condition that

- yes with equity

- yes with a convertible loan.

Obviously 'no' can cause offence (see Rule 100). 'Yes' is a no-no, if you see what I mean. Lending money to friends and family isn't on unless you are prepared to write it off (see Rule 97) and generally people who want big loans aren't that close or they'd know you better.

This leaves us with the last three – conditions, equity or convertible. There may be others of course.

- **Conditions.** A mug's game if you ask me. On the condition you repay me when you've made your fortune. Hmm. On the condition you don't do anything silly with this. Hmm. On the condition you only use this for the good of mankind. Hmm. Conditions is such a tricky one but there are many who'll ask for conditions – 'If you would just be so good as to lend me this I promise to...blah blah'. Yeah, right.

- **Equity.** Better. You don't lend, you offer to buy a share in whatever project it is. If it is successful you recoup with interest. If it fails, you shouldn't have been lending – or buying into it – in the first place. More fool you. The trouble with equity is that it's often black and white, hit or miss.

You get your money back if the project is successful – and perhaps that should be *when* the project is successful.

- **Convertible.** Much better. You lend as a proper loan with repayment details all worked out legally so it is a binding loan. But if the project is successful – it should be or you shouldn't be lending in the first place – you convert the loan into equity. This way you get your money back plus a big share of the profits. It sort of makes lending seem worthwhile.

If approached for a loan, asking for a convertible loan will sort the wheat from the chaff, the serious from the not so serious. It makes the serious stand up and be counted. If the project then fails you get your money back – in theory at least. Obviously if the project fails there may not be any money but you will have secured it against their property of course (I know I said never to do that, but that was advice for you as a borrower; as a lender always make sure you do). I even do this with my children if tempted to lend them any money for big items like cars and houses. Yes, you can have the money but I want to own a share, so you can't sell it if you get bored or restless or whatever without my permission. Amazing how often they back off when they know I'll be their partner. And I also then know that they did buy the item rather than something they'd rather not tell me about.

> ## ASKING FOR A CONVERTIBLE LOAN WILL SORT THE WHEAT FROM THE CHAFF

You really, really can't take it with you

I know there's a saying – whoever has the most toys at the end wins. But you really can't take it with you and you can't buy anything with it when you go – no tickets into heaven, no indulgences, no get-out-of-hell-free cards. When you go, you go alone and with nothing, just as you came in. So all that effort, in a way, is wasted. Unless of course you did something useful with it when you had it and had the ability to do it. Left drooling in some old folks' home isn't the time or place to start being philanthropic, is it?

Not getting rid of it is known as wealth bondage – being tied so tightly to your money that you really do try to take it with you – and that really is kinky. Sure you can leave it to your kids but you should have given most of it away long before you pop your clogs or you'll be leaving a massive tax liability for someone down the line.

> NOT GETTING RID OF
> IT IS KNOWN AS
> WEALTH BONDAGE

Whatever you decide to do, do take the proper advice – nothing grates so much as a poorly thought-out will and lots of tax after you've gone.

You can of course insure against tax liabilities after you've gone. You have to calculate what you think your tax liability is likely to be and then set up a whole-of-life insurance policy to cover it. But the policy has to be written into a trust to ensure the proceeds from the policy aren't included with your estate – but for heaven's sake be careful of placing anything in trust because if you use the wrong one you can make things even worse.

Gosh, I'm not a financial adviser (except on a behavioural level – you need somebody else for the nitty-gritty-which-investment-is-best-for-me detail) but it seems to make sense to have all this tied up before you go. And of course you can leave the lot to your spouse and then they don't have to pay death duties* but by golly their tax bill is going to be high when they go, so you are only delaying rather than off-setting – although the effect of this is reduced in the UK by the ability to claim a deceased spouse's unused nil rate bond. Alternatively, you can establish a trust to ensure that both husband and wife's nil rate bands are fully utilized – but again be very careful using a trust.

I was reading about the Dalai Lama's wealth the other day. He gets paid the equivalent of around 38p a day expenses, owns two robes – one on and one in the wash – and his only indulgence is a new watchstrap every now and again (I did wonder if he bought leather ones). And yet he is the head of an entire country – albeit one in exile. Now that is cool in my book.

---

* Spouse's exemption – it must be your spouse or civil partner and if they are domiciled outside the UK the exemption is restricted to £325,000.

Know when/how to say no – and yes

Now you've made some money there will be those who see you as:

- a target – easy pickings

- owing them something – after all, they have known you for years . . .

- worth taking a chance on – you never know

- a genuine source of low-interest loan or free gifts – and so much easier than preparing a proper business plan and going to the bank.

I'm not saying you will always get the outstretched hand. In fact some requests will be cloaked in the most attractive brochures of potential investments. So how do you know when to say yes and when to say no? And how to say either?

Saying no to friends and family is easy, in a sense. Right from day one you make it a policy – and a very easily identifiable one – not to lend to friends and family (see Rule 97). You never do, so they learn not to ask.

Saying no to business acquaintances is also easy. Just ask them to refer everything to your accountant or business adviser. Say you never make a decision without their input and you can't proceed until they have studied everything in close detail. That puts off the ones who are just arm-round-the-shoulder trying it on. The others might be worth considering if they have genuine plans. In which case it might be worth having a look.

Now, *when* to say yes or no. Say no if:

- your gut instinct says to say no

- they haven't done any work on their presentation – if they are lazy at ground zero it strikes me they'll be lazy right through

- you have no connection with them – always say no to strangers basically.

To say yes is fine. To say no is fine. It's your money and you can do with it what you want. You have to:

- Let go of any guilt – this is business.

- Make sure you understand exactly what is being asked for – that's why calling in advisers is always a good idea.

- Keep a closed-door policy to stop yourself being overwhelmed by requests – make it hard for them to get to you.

- Avoid saying yes because you think it will make people happy – they are emotionally blackmailing you and thus get themselves crossed off the list automatically and without guilt.

- Always be very clear when you are saying no. No 'maybes' or 'we'll see' or 'I'll have to sleep on that one'. Say no and put everyone out of their misery – including you.

- Don't allow yourself to be badgered. Be assertive.

- Stop them in their tracks – a simple 'I'd rather you didn't ask me' before they've even got started.

> # IT'S YOUR MONEY AND YOU CAN DO WITH IT WHAT YOU WANT

Find ways to give people money without them feeling they are in your debt

I love this one. It is such a challenge to give money to people who:

- haven't asked for it

- need it

- deserve it

- will use it wisely/well.

And the challenge is to get them to accept it without feeling indebted to you, beholden, grudging, guilty, whatever. This is one of those rules we all ought to practise no matter how much money we have. I reckon you get to start as soon as you become a parent and give your kids big money for cars and things. They are always saying 'I'll pay you back', and you know they won't. But if you can give them money without all that stuff being attached to it, you are doing well.

There are a variety of approaches to help you give your money away without them feeling guilty or you embarrassed:

- **You might win the lottery one day**. This is a good one as it implies that there, but for a bit of luck, you go. All they've got to do is be as lucky as you and they'll pay you back.

- **Fortunes change and they go down as well as up**. Basically what you are saying is that you are flush at the moment but that might not always be the case and when your fortunes go down, they can help you out.

- **I like my friends to be happy**. How can I be happy when I see my friends in misery/trouble/debt/whatever? If you aren't happy then I can't be, so I'll help myself to become happy by helping you to become happy. How can anyone refuse?

- **Why shouldn't I help my friends?** This is a subset of the one above but still valuable and useful. Look, it's what friends are for. You've helped me out in the past/are helping me by.../have always offered help anyway so why can't I do the same for you?

- **Help me out here, I've got a tax problem**. Look, if I can offload some of this cash I can alleviate my tax burden, so can you help me by taking some? I would be ever so grateful.

- **The taxman will only get it after I'm dead**. So can I give it to you now and see the pleasure it'll bring you rather than you be grieving and moping after I've gone?

- **Let me help with a housing upgrade by taking equity in the new house**. They pay nothing until they snuff it, at which point your investment will probably show better appreciation than the interest rate it would have earned on deposit. And if it doesn't, so what? Profit was never the point anyway, but they can feel happy about it.

I'm sure if you put your mind to it there will be many more you can come up with. Hey, this one is fun. You get to help others, give loads away, share your wealth and be creative all at the same time.

> IF YOU CAN GIVE THEM MONEY WITHOUT ALL THAT STUFF BEING ATTACHED TO IT, YOU ARE DOING WELL

Don't over-protect your children from the valuable experience of poverty

Look, if you're about to ask your parents for a really big loan (gift?) then you'd better buy up every copy of this book you can and burn the lot of them because you're not going to like what I have to say next.

Parents, if you are reading this then don't give them that loan (gift). It is OK not to mollycoddle them, to make them learn the value of money, to make them treat money with respect right from the word go. And just because you have lots doesn't mean they are entitled to stand there with their hand out right from the day they get out of nappies.

I'm the world's worst at this one but I am learning. There are various ways you can go from being utterly mean and not giving them a bean to being overly generous and giving them everything. Now, I was going to talk about setting budgets for children and setting up trust funds for them.

A monthly allowance is always a good idea as they then have to live within their means. It teaches them to budget and to scrimp and save at the end of the month – or halfway through it in most cases. When they first go off to uni is probably the best time to do this as they are also learning a whole new batch of things about being grown up – sex, drugs, staying out late, wrong sort of friends, binge drinking. Learning to balance their own books at the same time is good for them.

You can set aside lump sums for them as well so they can buy a house, business, decent car. If you administer it, then they can't blow it on a plasma TV or a £600 designer handbag but only a sensible thing that they have to explain to you in some detail. And of course a trust fund for when you have shuffled off. Or of course let them have such a fund when they are of an age sensible enough to enjoy it without it diverting them from their education. Personally, I would give it to them after it would make any real difference to them; in effect after they have started to earn their own money in worthwhile amounts.

And for goodness' sake don't ever tell them they are getting a lump sum aged 25 or whatever you decide. Nothing demotivates a child more than thinking they're coming into money. They'll think they don't have to make any effort. Let them think they'll always be poor and watch them go.

And how do you set a good allowance figure? Only you can work it out for your child and it obviously varies depending on age but once they reach their teens it's as well to thrash it out with them – a process sometimes of painful discussion (who said rows?). But make them argue every penny and justify it. It'll make them value it when they get to spend it.

> # A MONTHLY ALLOWANCE
> # IS ALWAYS A GOOD IDEA

Know how to choose charities/good causes

Once you have some money you get inundated with requests to give to charities. I'm not talking about the emotional black-mail ones we all get through the letterbox – these three pennies could pay for food for an entire family forever and a rainforest and sight for all the blind people in the world and all you have to do is send them back with whatever you can afford. Oh the guilt when you spend those three pennies – not!

I'm talking about big charitable donations, supporting a particular cause, sponsoring a particular person. I've always had my doubts – and this is entirely subjective, entirely personal – about supporting a penguin or endangered fish or threatened albatross. How do you know which is yours? In the zoo you can at least go and have a look at your own saved pet but in the wild it is so much more difficult.

Anyway here are a few tips for choosing a good charity – a good one for you:

- Decide what is important to you – the planet, saving whales, small children, the poor, cancer research.

- Work out what you want to do – just give money, get involved, be an adviser, raise funds (I've always wanted to drive one of those inflatables for Greenpeace; I just think those boats are so cool).

- Check out charities you might think suitable on the internet and see if your ideals fit in with theirs.

- Check out the charities themselves – financial statements, accounts, brochures, campaign information, membership, mission statements.

- Trust your gut feelings.

DECIDE WHAT IS IMPORTANT TO YOU

Personally I reject any charities that directly approach me. Not because it makes me cross but as a way of weeding out the ones I don't want to support. I have my own mission statements when it comes to charity giving and not being approached is part of that. I also like charities that set out to help directly instead of merely churning out aid – teaching villagers to fish and all that. I also only support small charities as I figure they need it more.

And I will only support small charities that are doing things that seem attainable. I figure feeding the poor of the world requires a bottomless pit. Not that it isn't a decent objective but one I find too remote. But one that seeks to provide fresh water for a particular village I can relate to; or providing a breakfast for an inner-city schoolkid.*

---

* www.magicbreakfast.com is something I *can* get my head round.

RULE 104

Spend your own money because no one will spend it as wisely as you

What! Surely we all spend our own money? No, we don't. As we get richer, the need to have others spend it for us grows stronger. Believe me, it becomes a real risk to hand things over and lose value and wealth because of it. It is so easy to figure that because we are busy and someone offers, it is a good thing to hand over.

I have noticed that the successful rich don't hand over anything; they carry on paying attention to detail all the time. Obviously there might come a time to hand over as we grow too old to administer our own affairs but until then, give up nothing.

> I HAVE NOTICED THAT THE
> SUCCESSFUL RICH DON'T
> HAND OVER ANYTHING

Examples? Of course. I have a friend who has considerable wealth and who is happy to hand over his spending to anyone around him who offers to do it for him. His gardener buys all his equipment, including mowers and chain saws and the like. Top of the range? I should say. This gardener is driving around on mowers that are the gardening equivalent of a Rolls Royce. My friend just signs the cheques and the gardener is laughing all the way to the tool shed. My friend also pays caterers to come in and organize meals every time he wants to entertain. Again he signs the cheque and the caterers supply him with a complete dinner party.

Ah, but I hear you say, 'So what? He can afford it.' Yes, indeed he can but he is also:

- being ripped off repeatedly
- not getting good value for money
- slowly losing control over his own financial affairs
- losing the respect of his employees and hired service companies who see him as a bit of a joke – too much money and not enough sense.

He's the same when it comes to buying a new car. He just rings up the showroom and they deliver what he wants. Trouble is they frequently deliver what they've had sitting in their showrooms for too long and can't shift. Ask him about the pink Bentley he bought that no one else was going to touch in a million years. I tease him and ask him if the showroom had a big glass office where they could sit and see him coming.

You've got to retain control of your own spending if you want to retain control over your finances – and dignity. No pink Bentleys for you. Don't hand out credit cards. Don't give anyone authority to sign personal cheques. Don't use a personal shopper. Set people proper budgets. Get them to submit proper proposals for spending. Check the small print. Check everything. Question everything. Stay on top. Stay in control. And if you want my advice – no joint accounts, ever. There's no need for it in this day and age.

Take responsibility before you take advice

This is a follow-on from the previous Rule. If you are going to take advice you need to know in advance:

- what you expect to get

- why you are asking

- your exact position – if you don't know, how can they advise you of anything?

- what you want to happen next

- what role the adviser will play in that

- what action you can take if their advice is wrong/out of date/ harmful

- what further advice you might need.

And before you can do any of these you need to take responsibility.

We all start out – or at least I did, and so did most people I've ever talked to about it – somehow expecting that we would end up rich. It was/is an assumed process, sort of by osmosis. As you get older and add years to your life, so in theory you add riches. Then you wake up one day and it isn't/is just like that. For me it wasn't, so I went into hyperdrive to change the situation and am now fabulously wealthy.* But it took hard work and tremendous effort. Now you've made it, it is time to review. Time to take responsibility. Time to take stock.

---

* If you are the tax collector I was only joking and/or I've already paid my tax bill.

You need to know:

- where you are

- how you got there

- what you are worth – both financially and spiritually

- where you want to go next

- how you expect to get there.

When you have answered these questions you are ready to take advice about your plans. And it doesn't have to be advice of the paid kind, the expert kind, the man-in-a-suit kind, the all serious and heavy kind. Sometimes advice can come from unlikely sources and unlikely people. Learn to listen. Learn to take in what is *not* being said. Learn to be happy (gosh, that's a big one for all of us).

The wealthier we become, the easier it appears to be to hand over our affairs (financial ones) to people we think have our best interests at heart or who we assume know what they are doing or are on top of the latest developments and laws. My observation is that (a) they're not and (b) the shrewd wealthy ones don't hand over anything unless they are really, really sure of their advisers. And that's my advice.

> SOMETIMES ADVICE
> CAN COME FROM
> UNLIKELY SOURCES AND
> UNLIKELY PEOPLE

RULE 106

Once you've got it, don't flaunt it

Wealth is lovely. Having money is great. Getting rich is a worthwhile and enjoyable activity. Buying the pink Bentley is just plain gross. As is a lot of other things that shout nouveau riche, over-the-top, flaunting, bling. So tacky. Take lessons in how to handle wealth by all means but do handle it well.

I read a nice story the other day of a young lad who got to stay in a millionaire's mansion – a relative I assume – and when he went to bed he left the light on. The millionaire popped his head round the door and told him it was wasting money and he should turn it off. He even threatened him with a $1 fine. But instead he tossed him a $1 coin and turned the light out himself. The kid never forgot the incident and is still turning lights off when he goes to bed or leaves a room to this day. And he still doesn't know why the reverse psychology worked. As he says, he went from a possible $1 fine to a big windfall (it was 1953 when a dollar was a lot).

Be frugal. Be careful with your money. Don't flaunt it. And as you now belong to an exclusive club, could you please observe a few rules:

- no flash cars
- no castles, ranches or ranch-style house – this isn't Dallas you know
- no bling
- no glitz or showing off
- no impulse spending
- no wild animals as pets
- no buying islands
- no private jets

- no flying all your relatives to a foreign country for a party

- no flying your relatives to a foreign country for your latest trophy wedding

- no huge diamonds – or big jewellery of any sort, it'll only attract the robbers and thieves.

Be a discreet, tasteful, refined, cultured, less-is-more, more-is-tacky, quiet sort of rich person. Someone we can all look up to. Someone who will inspire and not cultivate ridicule – they do laugh at those leopard skin trousers I'm afraid (not that you've got any). Someone who will set a good example to the young, the impressionable, the not so well-off.

We've all seen those who come into money too suddenly and flaunt the fact that they have loads and we all think 'God, how tacky'. I know we shouldn't sit in judgement on others but I do find my toes curl at . . . no, I can't say in case you've got one.

Flaunting it creates envy, jealousy (different from envy), criticism, snobbery, condemnation, censure – and all quite rightly. Discretion, on the other hand, encourages respect, admiration and emulation. Don't ever mention how much you've got, what you are worth or how much you earn. Ever. If you tell people, half will despise you for not having more and the other half resent you for having so much. Only reveal such information to your bank manager and even then they should have to drag the info from you.

DON'T EVER MENTION HOW MUCH YOU'VE GOT, WHAT YOU ARE WORTH OR HOW MUCH YOU EARN

What's next? Pacts with the devil?

We're near the end of the Rules and I guess we can have some fun. Creating wealth is as varied and different an adventure for each of us as anything else. We can work for it, win the lottery or a poker game (mind you, it would have to be a pretty big one), inherit it, steal it, be awarded it as a prize (Nobel Prize for literature – you do get around $1.1 million.* Gulp. Put my name forward at once please, somebody. Or what about the Templeton Prize, which gets you $1.6 million**), or find it in the street (lots of examples on the internet of people finding huge wads of cash), marry into it, you name it. And of course if you are really desperate there is the old pact with the devil – but beware of gotcha clauses.

The Chinese believe, via feng shui, that if you leave your loo seat up, your money will get flushed away. I wonder if this is a modern invention because I have no evidence of flushing loos in China when feng shui was being established in the Taoist eras.

Then there are affirmations – you write down the wealth you want and pin it up so you can see it every day and chant it out hundreds of times. Might work.

Then there's the cosmic ordering service – you tell the great cosmic bank how much it owes you and it repays you immediately – there has got to be a catch there somewhere knowing banks; they're all the same I reckon.

---

* 8 million Swedish krona – the actual value changes with fluctuating currency conversion rates.
** The Templeton Prize is awarded annually by an international, multifaith panel of judges to a living person of any religious tradition who has made a unique contribution to progress in research or discoveries about spiritual realities.

THERE IS THE OLD PACT WITH THE DEVIL – BUT BEWARE OF GOTCHA CLAUSES

Then there's crystals – you wear one/sleep with it/carry it around. Certain crystals resonate with the cosmic bank (them again) and it's a sort of rock cheque I guess.*

Dowsing? You follow hazel rods (or bits of bent coat hangers and empty Biros depending on which books you read) which twitch when you are above buried treasure or a seam of gold or one of those ring-pull things off the top of a beer can. Bit like a metal detector but doesn't need batteries.

I suppose you could buy a racehorse but it seems so very risky to me. Laying down fine wines? Could work but I couldn't resist the temptation I think.

I am not scoffing at any of these methods. However, you intend gaining prosperity, you should get on with it, believe in it, follow it, give 100 per cent to it and not listen to others. Including me. Especially me. Good luck.

---

* Citrine, ruby and tiger eye are supposed to work but I figure if you can buy rubies you don't need the wealth or you're giving it all to the crystal seller, so I suppose it works for them.

THE RULES OF
OTHER PEOPLE'S
WEALTH

As you've read nearly all this book, I think it's safe to assume that money is something you want to have more of. All well and good, but time for a note of caution: if money is important to you, your attitude to *other people's* money will have a big impact on your overall satisfaction with life. Especially when they choose to do things with money that directly affect you. Whether it's your children's money, your parents' money, your friends' money – you need to make yourself pretty immune to other people's decisions in order to avoid a great deal of heartache, upset and even hurt.

So the Rules that follow are designed to help you handle your attitude to other people's wealth while you're building up your own. You don't want to become wracked and knotted with jealousy, frustration, stress, bile and misery while you watch other people make stupid mistakes (or at least what you consider to be stupid mistakes) with the money they have and you covet.

No, you want to be able to separate your own fortunes from those of everyone around you, so that you don't take their financial decisions personally, or get hung up on how they spend their money. Then you can simply resolve to do the right thing when it comes to your own wealth, and other people's decisions will be nothing to do with you. It's easier said than done, but I hope the Rules that follow will help you.

Don't judge

I remember meeting a friend of a friend once, who I knew was seriously rich. We were invited to a party at his house and you could see from the minute you turned off the road how wealthy he was, before you even caught sight of the house. As a matter of fact, he was titled as well as rich – minor aristocracy. Very fancy. I'll admit that the inverted snob in me had already decided I wouldn't much like him. Out of touch, arrogant, privileged – oh yes, I'd pre-judged him utterly before we ever actually met.

Of course, when I was introduced to him (surprise, surprise) he turned out to be a lovely chap. Down-to-earth, empathetic, amusing, a great listener. I know it's clichéd but it's still so easy to walk into the trap of judging people by their money. I was the one being predictable, whereas he was just being himself.

That particular man was born into money and privilege. Most of us have a slightly different view of people who have come from a more ordinary background and acquired money later in life. There are lots of terms for them, all of which carry slightly pejorative overtones: self-made, nouveau riche, new money. Again, we make judgements about these people before we even know them. There are plenty of clichés here too: more money than sense, no taste, full of themselves. And again, the vast majority of these people don't fit this description at all.

If we make assumptions about people because of the money they have – earned, inherited or otherwise acquired – it's us who deserve to be harshly judged. We're the ones behaving predictably. Lots of wealthy people give away stacks of money to good causes. Not all of them will shout about it though, so you might not even know. Many of them are completely grounded people who do understand what life is like for the rest of us. Most of them are as sensible with their wealth as you or I would like to be in their position.

I don't assume that everyone I meet who has little or no money is automatically bound to be a good person, so why should I assume that someone with lots of money is a bad person? If (lack of) money has no influence on people's basic nature, why should having money change them? Of course money changes a few people for the worse, but then fame or kids or promotion or alcohol can do that too. Most people are just themselves, whether they happen to have loads or nothing at all. So let's just see them for who they are and not for what they have.

> **IF WE MAKE ASSUMPTIONS ABOUT PEOPLE BECAUSE OF THE MONEY THEY HAVE, IT'S US WHO DESERVE TO BE HARSHLY JUDGED**

Don't envy it

It's hard to look at wealthy people in the public eye and not wish you had what they have. Mind you, you don't necessarily know what else they have that goes with the money – they may have all kinds of personal problems or hidden angst you wouldn't want, not to mention the direct effects of money such as being chased around interminably by paparazzi, or being obliged to live in three houses at once, which I always think must be horrible.*

Yes, it's tough to watch and wish. Ah, but that's nothing to how tough it is when the person with all the money isn't some distant celebrity but your best friend, your neighbour, your colleague, your sister... Now that gets really tough to cope with. In fact the closer they are, the harder it is. If the couple next door don't seem to do much work yet have three overseas holidays a year, while you're working all hours and can't justify a week in Skegness, it can be pretty hard to bear.

I knew someone who cut off all contact with her best friend, much as she loved her, because she simply couldn't cope with her own jealousy as her friend grew slowly wealthier over the years, while her own fortunes dwindled. It was very sad. She ended up no wealthier, and now she'd given up her best friend as well. But that's not all. The best friend went on to suffer a terrible personal tragedy, which she would gladly have given all her money to avoid, which is my main point.

You see, if you don't have money, you can imagine it's the answer to everything. You know, 'If only I had a six figure annual income, everything would be perfect'. But it isn't, you see. Which means that while you're busy envying wealthy

---

* 'Where are my favourite socks?' 'Has anyone seen my glasses? I definitely remember having them in Paris...' 'I must walk the dog. Hang on, where is the dog? Actually, did you remember to bring the kids?'

people for their money, they're busy envying other people (maybe even you) for their marriage, or their health, or their sporting accomplishments, or the fact that their job is so rewarding. Listen, we can all find things to envy in others, however poor or wealthy we are. Or we can be grateful for everything we have and build on it, instead of hankering after what other people have got.

> **WHILE YOU'RE BUSY ENVYING WEALTHY PEOPLE FOR THEIR MONEY, THEY'RE BUSY ENVYING OTHER PEOPLE**

RULE 3

Other people's money belongs to them

When you read in your daily newspaper that some celebrity has spent a fortune on yet another mansion, or invested part of their wealth in an exciting new project, or given away millions to charity, the odds are that you think it's up to them if they want to be stupid/generous/take risks. You shrug and move on to the next story, or maybe turn to the financial pages to find some ideas for making your own fortune.

It's harder when it's your parents though, isn't it? Or your friend, sibling, work colleague, neighbour? Suppose your brother decides to spend all his savings on buying a holiday home, or your best friend wants to plough all their money into some business idea you think will crash, or your parents want to make a big donation to a charity that's special to them, or your colleague wants to spend thousands on cosmetic surgery that you don't think they even need. Are you still going to shrug and turn the page?

Sometimes it's not easy. For a start you need to remember a key Rule, 'Never give advice unless it's asked for'. That can be difficult enough. After all, you might be really concerned that these people are making a terrible mistake. But, you know, you might be wrong. Maybe if your brother never uses his holiday home, he'll still be able to sell it at a profit. Perhaps your colleague will gain huge confidence from the surgery, even if you can't see why.

Maybe your reservations aren't about making bad financial decisions. Perhaps you just think these are irresponsible things to do with money.

Actually, the reason is irrelevant – it doesn't matter what you think. People are allowed to be irresponsible with their money if they want to. It's theirs. Maybe they don't approve of some of your choices, but you don't want them telling you so, because it's none of their business. You may think they are profligate with their money – while they might think that you're a Scrooge who has no idea how to enjoy what you have because you're too busy making more of it. But they don't say so (I hope).

So there are two things here. The first, and I hope the easiest, is about keeping your mouth shut unless you're asked for an opinion. If you are asked, you can say what you think but don't be fooled into supposing that gives you the right to put pressure on people to accept your advice. They may listen and then disregard it, and that's their prerogative.

The second thing is about what you actually think privately. It's not enough just to keep quiet. You also need to understand properly that it's none of your business what other people do with their money. You might think, 'Well, I wouldn't have done that', which is fine. But don't judge, or get emotionally involved. Why? Partly because you wouldn't want other people judging you, and partly because the sooner you stop fretting over stuff that's nothing to do with you, the sooner you can focus on your own life. And that's got to be good.

> **PEOPLE ARE ALLOWED TO BE IRRESPONSIBLE WITH THEIR MONEY IF THEY WANT TO**

RULE 4

They can give it all away if they like

Following on from the last Rule, not only can other people be irresponsible with their money, they can get rid of the lot if they want to. They can give it away, gamble it, burn it, spend it on sweets. They can do as they please. Yes, even your parents.

What? Your money? Your parents can just be allowed to give away your inheritance? Well no, actually, that would be impossible, because it isn't your inheritance until they've gone. If they're still here and capable of spending it, it's not *your* inheritance. It's *their* money. Just like your money is yours.

I understand that this can be very tough. Especially if you're in a financial black hole and the only way out of the pit that you can see is the money you're expecting from your parents when they go. And when other people's parents are being careful with *their* money so they can pass it on, it's doubly frustrating if your parents choose to spend all theirs.

Which is precisely why you have to understand, to grasp, to believe in your heart and not just your head, that it's their right to spend it. Otherwise watching them fritter money away – or even donate it all to a good cause – can sour your relationship with your parents and burn you up with anger.

But look, just because you had your eye on the money, doesn't make it yours. Why should they have to stop enjoying themselves, just to save up for you? Especially if you're still able to earn after they've retired? And at what age do you think *your* money should stop being yours and become your children's? When should *you* stop being allowed to do anything fun or interesting – if it costs money – so that your wealth can be protected for someone else? If you don't expect the principle to apply to you in due course, you certainly can't apply it to your parents. Once they've gone, no amount of money will bring them back.

So let them enjoy it while they still can. Even if – especially if – you have the kind of parents who mess you about emotionally, who tell you they're leaving you everything and then change their minds and spend it...even if they led you to believe it was 'your' money...even so, don't listen to them. It's their money, all theirs, just for them, exclusively, until the day they die. If after that you find there's something left for you, just be grateful.

> ## THEY CAN GIVE IT AWAY, GAMBLE IT, BURN IT, SPEND IT ON SWEETS

RULE 5a

Once they've gone, you can't ask questions

If you can master Rule 4, it might make this one a little bit easier. It's very common for parents to die and not split their money equally between their children and/or grandchildren. And when it happens, they're not there to give you an explanation. So you probably assume that they never loved you as much as your brother or sister, the other side of the family or something of the kind.

Look, there are lots of reasons why parents might love their children equally, but not split the money equally. Probably the most common of these are that, in their eyes:

- one of the children needs the money much more
- one of the children has been given much more already
- one of the children has done far more for them.

Of course, there might be some other reason. But the thing is that parents often don't discuss these things in advance. Maybe they don't want to start a family argument, or maybe they're worried they'll be put under pressure to change their will. For whatever reason, you may not get a chance to ask what's going on.

The way to deal with this starts with Rule 4 – you have to fully embrace the fact that it's their money and they can do as they please with it. Then recognize that they may not have thought as you do. So how did they think? What would have been their reasoning? Unless you come from a highly dysfunctional family (I'll come to that), the answer will almost always be that it seemed right and logical to them.

Now you have to find their logic – get your head round their way of thinking – so that you can understand how your parents could do this without it being a reflection on their love for you. Perhaps they were short sighted in not seeing how you'd feel, but they weren't thinking of you in isolation, they were trying to find what seemed to them a fair balance between all their children. This obviously doesn't help you financially, but frankly the emotional fallout of this kind of thing can be far worse than the financial hardship. After all, you haven't actually lost money, you've simply not gained money that you probably know, deep down, you shouldn't really have let yourself rely on.

What matters is that you aren't left resenting your parents instead of cherishing the memory of them. It won't help to be bitter. It may take time, and you may need to talk to other people to help you through it, but you need to reach a point where you understand your parents' motives even if you don't agree with them. Look at your siblings from your parents' perspective and not your own. And in time you'll find you can accept the decision without rancour.

> **THERE ARE LOTS OF REASONS WHY PARENTS MIGHT LOVE THEIR CHILDREN EQUALLY, BUT NOT SPLIT THE MONEY EQUALLY**

Once they've gone, you can't ask questions

OK, here's the opposite situation, and this one happens loads too. You have struggled with money for years, with a family to support, while your sister has a high-paid job and no kids. And what do your parents do? They split their money equally, even though your sister barely needs her share and your half still leaves you with pretty shaky finances.

Or how about this: your parents were unwell for years, and you gave up weekends and even took holiday entitlement to look after them, take them to hospital appointments, mow the lawn for them, help with their shopping, cleaning, accounts and all the rest. Meanwhile your brother was living on the other side of the world and visited once every couple of years, and maybe phoned occasionally (far too infrequently probably). And after all that, when the second parent finally dies, you find they've left you half of everything each. Yes, he got as much as you.

After all you've done! How could they? Ah, but you didn't do it in the expectation of a reward, did you? You did it because you loved them and you wanted to do it. I know that because you're a Rules Player. If you'd been the kind of person to do it simply for the payoff at the end, I'm not sure you'd have deserved it anyway.

Here's what you have to understand. For many people, the way they divide up their assets in their will has very little to do with the money itself. It's about what it symbolizes. And their will is the last chance for them to show their children how much they mean to them. If they love them both/all equally, they feel they have to split the will equally. They worry about the scenario we looked at in Rule 5a. And the one we're coming to in Rule 6.*

---

* No, don't turn the page! Patience!

If they love you the same, they can't see any option but to show it in the way they divide up their estate.

And besides, you have to remember that your parents don't see your brother or sister from a sibling perspective. They're a loving, forgiving parent. Perhaps, in their eyes, it was your choice to give up your career to have a family while your sister stayed childless and focused on her career. Or, in the other example, they accepted your brother's decision to move abroad – it was what he wanted for a better life for his family, and however much they missed him, they brought you both up to have free will, to make your own choices and they won't punish either of you for that.

What matters most of all here is that you don't resent your siblings for the choices that your parents made. Think that one through, and you'll see how illogical it is. Not only illogical, but also deeply divisive. And that certainly isn't what divide-it-all-equally parents want.

> **THE WAY PEOPLE DIVIDE UP THEIR ASSETS IN THEIR WILL HAS VERY LITTLE TO DO WITH THE MONEY ITSELF**

Blood comes before money

I said I'd mention very dysfunctional families. Sadly, a few parents don't care what emotional wreckage they leave when they die, and may even design their will to create hurt or dissension. If this applies to you, you'll know because they'll have been doing it for long years before they finally go. They may well have promised the same things to you and your siblings, or tried to manipulate you with threats about what you will or won't get in their will.

At least if this is the case, you probably had no expectations anyway, but you may have had hopes that are dashed when it comes to it. Mind you, there are plenty of other, less obviously dysfunctional parents who make disruptive decisions about who to leave everything to.

I used to know a man whose father was furious with him for shaving his head (seems strange to me, but that's folks for you). So furious, in fact, that in a fit of pique the father cut his son out of his will. And then the father died suddenly and unexpectedly before he could calm down and rethink.

I have one friend, with five siblings, who came from a very traditional family. His mother died first and, when his dad died, he left absolutely everything to my friend. Why? Because he was the eldest son, and as far as his dad was concerned, the eldest son should inherit everything. Now in some cultures that may still be true, but in London about 20 years ago it certainly wasn't the norm.

Part of the problem here, obviously, is that you don't end up inheriting what you'd hoped to. But that's not generally the biggest issue. The real difficulty is what happens to your relationships with your brothers or sisters when one or other of you feels that your siblings are benefiting at your expense.

We touched on this in the last Rule, and the first thing to grasp is that your siblings didn't ask for this any more than you did. If your parents' will (or indeed your grandparents' will, or any other will that benefits some of the family more than others) creates bad feeling within families, you're all victims. Whether your parents intended it or simply didn't think things through, everyone is in a difficult position. The sibling that comes off best generally feels guilty and uncomfortable, and under pressure to give away money that their parents expressly wanted them to have. The sibling that misses out on the money may feel they're the only loser, but that's not true.

And it's rarely that cut and dried. The sibling with the lion's share of the inheritance may feel that they need it more, or deserve it more, or have had less until now. You may disagree but the point is that it's often a matter of opinion. Clearly your parents thought, for whatever reason, that one sibling should have most.

If your relationship with your brother or sister was previously even half-decent, saving that relationship is far more important than the money, and potentially far more valuable. Sooner or later most of us hit bad times, and there are countless circumstances where money doesn't help one jot, but the support of family will be worth the world to you. Remember that.

> **THE REAL DIFFICULTY IS WHAT HAPPENS TO YOUR RELATIONSHIPS WITH YOUR BROTHERS OR SISTERS**

Your children owe you nothing

Right. That's enough about your parents' money. Now, what about your children's cash? Suppose you've struggled all your life, and they've done really well for themselves. In fact, the reason you've struggled is because you were supporting them, and their success is in large part down to the sacrifices you made to give them the best start you could.

And now they're in a position to make your life a little bit easier. That's not too much to ask, is it? They could give you a bit of money, or help towards the bills, or treat you to a nice holiday, after all you've done for them.

I hope you know pretty much what I'm going to say. No. I repeat, that's a big fat no. Don't you dare ask your children for money. And while we're at it, don't even imply that they should consider giving you some. If you think back all those years, it was your choice (or possibly your carelessness) that brought them into the world, and they never signed any kind of agreement. You *wanted* to give them a good start, create a supportive home, make sure their childhood was comfortable. Those were all your choices.

I'm certainly not suggesting they were bad choices. On the contrary, I congratulate you on giving your child the confidence and drive to do so well for themselves. But your reward is seeing your beloved child so successful. I don't believe that all the time you were kissing their grazed knees better, or helping with their homework, or listening to them sob about broken friendships, or cooking their meals, or picking up after them, that you were mentally counting off the value of it all in terms of what you could claim back from them when they were old enough to earn a living.

Listen, here's how it works. Your parents did all that stuff for you. You owe them nothing. Then you put in all the graft for your kids. They do it for their kids, and so on down the generations. We all get, and we all give. But we don't give back up the generations, we pass it on down. Your child's money is their own, and if you've set a good example, and they choose to have kids, they'll have learnt how to pass it on. That's your reward.

Of course, if you've done a good job of instilling the best values in your children, and with a bit of luck on your side, they may give you as much financial support as you hope for and more. Just as I hope you support your own parents in whatever way you can. One thing I can tell you though, from frequent observation: the more you ask for the less you're likely to get, and your children will resent you (and I'm including emotional blackmail there, as well as direct requests). Whereas if you don't ask, anything they give you will be given willingly and with love.

> # DON'T YOU DARE
> # ASK YOUR CHILDREN
> # FOR MONEY

RULE 8

Don't make money taboo

Conversations about money are tricky. I don't really know why this should be, but it's true – at least in most cultures. Absurdly, we find it difficult to talk about money even with our nearest and dearest. Now, most of the time this really doesn't matter. We've all learnt to find ways to achieve most of what we need without having to have those embarrassing, sordid, cringey, uncomfortable conversations.

OK, that's fine, but you've got to recognize when it becomes a problem. And I'm especially thinking about your parents as they get older. If they have any kind of money worries, you need to be able to support them. And you can't do that if neither they nor you feel you can even raise the subject.

Think about it. Once they're no longer earning, they have no idea how long the money they have will need to last. To put it bluntly, they don't know how long they've got before they die. So they have to look after their money carefully. That includes deciding if and when to sell their house if they own it, whether to go into a care home and what they can afford, when to start drawing any personal pension they may have, and so on.

Can they afford to go on holiday? Can they, indeed, afford to turn on the heating next winter? These decisions are really tough because they don't have all the information they need – i.e. how long they have to make the money last – so it's impossible to make a clear choice. Mostly they're operating on guesswork. Think how worrying that must be.

And you can help. But only if you know what's going on. Whether the help you can offer is in the form of money or advice, or reassurance that you'd never let them end up on the streets, you are their best source of help. They may not be up-to-date with all the financial options. They may not be good at that stuff anyway. They may even be a bit confused.

I have a friend whose father came from the pre-war generation, which meant that you didn't talk about personal stuff – you know, feelings, religion, worries, money. Her father was a bright man who, due to circumstances, was forced to leave school early and never fulfilled his intellectual potential. Instead he had a succession of low-paid jobs, and a period of unemployment. He spent all his life worrying deeply about money and 'being very careful', as it's known. He and his wife had very few luxuries and went for the budget option in pretty much everything. When he died, at a respectably old age, my friend was staggered to discover that he had been saving an excessively high proportion of his income for many years. My friend couldn't help but think about how much easier life would have been for her parents if her father hadn't been saving to this extent, during years of very low income.

Wouldn't it have been worth risking a tricky conversation to review their finances with them and encourage them to enjoy a little more of their hard-earned income? In fact, it's only broaching the subject that's uncomfortable. The worst that can happen is they say 'No thanks, we're fine', in which case you accept that and move on. Chances are, that they will appreciate your concern and once you're underway it will be fine, and they may be deeply relieved to be able to talk it through with you. So when the time comes, don't dither, just do it.

> # YOU CAN HELP. BUT ONLY IF YOU KNOW WHAT'S GOING ON

If they give it to you, it's yours

I think we've pretty much established by now that other people's money belongs entirely to them, to do with as they please. So it follows that you can do as you like with your own money.

But where did your money come from? Does that make a difference? It shouldn't, but for some people it does. If you've earned it through your own graft, you're probably fairly comfortable with making your own decisions about what to do with it. Ah, but what if it was given to you by someone else?

I've known people tie themselves in knots worrying about whether it's OK to do this or that with money given to them by family or friends, or inherited from someone who isn't even alive any longer to see how they spend it.

Let's be clear. If someone gives you money it not only becomes yours legally, but also morally, emotionally, psychologically. That's what a gift is. If someone gives you a birthday present of, let's say, a framed painting, do you feel obliged to consider which wall they would hang it on? If they gave you a bottle of perfume or aftershave, would you check with them before using it? No. Of course not. And money is just the same.

It's a different matter if you've been lent the money, or given it for a specific purpose. If your parents say, 'We'd like to give you some money to go on holiday', you'd either use it to go on holiday, or you'd discuss with them whether it would be OK to use it for something else. If your friend lends you money to set up a business, you don't go out and buy a sports car instead. But I'm talking about gifts of money, freely given, to be yours.

Some very non-Rules parents (this wouldn't be you) give their children money as a means of control. They proffer it as a gift, and then make remarks later about 'If I'd known you were going to waste it on this...' or 'Is that what you've done with our money?' They think that because the money came from them, they have a right to oversee what you do with it. Well, they don't, not if there were no conditions attached at the time they gave it to you. So don't let them guilt-trip you. You can choose whether to take the money, knowing what they'll say and whether your choices will influence future gifts. But that is a pragmatic decision, with no room for guilt.

So no matter how other people's money becomes your money, once it's in your hands/wallet/bank account, it's yours, and you're free to do as you please with it. Spend it or save it, but – either way – enjoy it.

> **IF SOMEONE GIVES YOU MONEY IT NOT ONLY BECOMES YOURS LEGALLY, BUT ALSO MORALLY, EMOTIONALLY, PSYCHOLOGICALLY**

HAD
ENOUGH
YET…?

Hey, it's not only wealth you know. If you're smart, you'll want to learn how the most successful people behave at whatever it is: life, money, work, relationships, kids. Luckily I've done the hard work for you – the years of observing, distilling, sieving and summarizing what really makes a difference into handy little Rules.

I've always been anxious not to stretch the Rules principle too far, but following huge demand from readers I have tackled those big important areas that affect us all. So in the pages that follow you'll find a 'one Rule' taster of each of the other Rules books:

Rules of Life
Rules of Work
Rules of Management
Rules of Parenting
Rules of Love

See what you think. And if you like them there are plenty more in each of the books.

You'll get older but not necessarily wiser

There is an assumption that as we get older we will get wiser; not true I'm afraid. The rule is we carry on being just as daft, still making plenty of mistakes. It's just that we make new ones, different ones. We do learn from experience and may not make the same mistakes again, but there is a whole new pickle jar of fresh ones just lying in wait for us to trip up and fall into. The secret is to accept this and not to beat yourself up when you do make new ones. The Rule really is: be kind to yourself when you do muck things up. Be forgiving and accept that it's all part of that growing older but no wiser routine.

Looking back, we can always see the mistakes we made, but we fail to see the ones looming up. Wisdom isn't about not making mistakes, but about learning to escape afterwards with our dignity and sanity intact.

When we are young, ageing seems to be something that happens to, well, old people. But it does happen to us all and we have no choice but to embrace it and roll with it. Whatever we do and whoever we are, the fact is we are going to get older. And this ageing process does seem to speed up as we get older.

You can look at it this way – the older you get, the more areas you've covered to make mistakes in. There will always be new areas of experience where we have no guidelines and where we'll handle things badly, overreact, get it wrong. And the more flexible we are, the more adventurous, the more life-embracing, then the more new avenues there will be to explore – and make mistakes in of course.

As long as we look back and see where we went wrong and resolve not to repeat such mistakes, there is little else we need to do. Remember that any Rules that apply to you also apply to everyone else around you. They are all getting older too. And not any wiser particularly. Once you accept this, you'll be more forgiving and kinder towards yourself and others.

Finally, yes, time does heal and things do get better as you get older. After all, the more mistakes you've made, the less likely that you'll come up with new ones. The best thing is that if you get a lot of your mistakes over and done with early on in life, there will be less to learn the hard way later on. And that's what youth is all about, a chance to make all the mistakes you can and get them out of the way.

WISDOM ISN'T ABOUT NOT MAKING MISTAKES BUT ABOUT LEARNING TO ESCAPE AFTERWARDS WITH OUR DIGNITY AND SANITY INTACT

Get your work noticed

It's all too easy for your work to get overlooked in the busy hurly burly of office life. You're slaving away and it can be hard to remember that you need to put in some effort to boost your individual status and personal kudos for your work. But it's important. You have to make your mark so you stand out and your promotional potential will be realized.

The best way to do this is to step outside the normal working routine. If you have to process so many widgets each day – and so does everyone else – then processing more won't do you that much good. But if you submit a report to your boss of how everyone could process more widgets then you'll get noticed. The unsolicited report is a brilliant way to stand out from the crowd. It shows you're thinking on your feet and using your initiative. But it mustn't be used too often. If you subject your boss to a barrage of unsolicited reports, you'll get noticed but in completely the wrong way. You have to stick to certain rules:

- Only submit a report occasionally.

- Make really sure that your report will actually work – that it will do good or provide benefits.

- Make sure your name is prominently displayed.

- Make sure the report will be seen not only by your boss, but by their boss as well.

- Remember it doesn't have to be a report – it can be an article in the company newsletter.

Of course, the very best way to get your work noticed is to be very, very good at your job. And the best way to be good at your job is to be totally dedicated to doing the job and ignoring all the rest. There is a vast amount of politics, gossip, gamesmanship, time wasting and socializing that goes on in the name of work. It isn't work. Keep your eye on the ball and you'll already be playing with a vast advantage over your colleagues. The Rules Player stays focused. Keep your mind on the task at hand – being very good at your job – and don't get distracted.

> THE UNSOLICITED REPORT IS
> A BRILLIANT WAY TO STAND
> OUT FROM THE CROWD

Get them emotionally involved

You manage people. People who are paid to do a job. But if it is 'just a job' to them, you'll never get their best. If they come to work looking to clock in and clock off and do as little as they can get away with in between, then you're doomed to failure, my friend. On the other hand, if they come to work looking to enjoy themselves, looking to be stretched, challenged, inspired and to get involved, then you are in with a big chance of getting the very best out of them. Trouble is, the jump from drudge to super team is entirely down to you. It is you that has to inspire them, lead them, motivate them, challenge them, get them emotionally involved.

That's OK. You like a challenge yourself, don't you? The good news is that getting a team emotionally involved is easy. All you have to do is make them care about what they are doing. And that's easy too. You have to get them to see the relevance of what they are doing, how it makes an impact on people's lives, how they provide the needs of other human beings, how they can reach out and touch people by what they do at work. Get them convinced – because it is true of course – that what they do makes a difference, that it contributes to society in some way rather than just lines the owner's or shareholder's pockets, or ensures that the chief executive gets a big fat pay cheque.

And yes. I know it's easier to show how they contribute if you manage nurses rather than an advertising sales team, but if you think about it, then you can find value in any role and instil pride in those who do whatever job it is. Prove it? OK. Well, those who sell advertising space are helping other companies, some of which may be very small, reach their markets. They are alerting potential customers to things they may have wanted for a long time and may really need. They are keeping the newspaper or magazine afloat as it relies on ad sales income, and that magazine or newspaper delivers information and/or gives pleasure to the people who buy it (otherwise they wouldn't, would they?).

Get them to care because that's an easy thing to do. Look, this is a given. Everyone deep down wants to be valued and to be useful. The cynics will say this is nonsense, but it is true, deep down true. All you have to do is reach down far enough and you will find care, feeling, concern, responsibility and involvement. Drag all that stuff up and they'll follow you forever and not even realize why.

Oh, just make sure that you've convinced yourself first before you try this out on your team. Do you believe that what you do makes a positive difference? If you're not sure, reach down, deep down, and find a way of caring...

> **GET THEM CONVINCED –**
> **BECAUSE IT IS TRUE OF**
> **COURSE – THAT WHAT THEY**
> **DO MAKES A DIFFERENCE**

Relax

So who are the best parents you know? The ones who have a seemingly instinctive ability to say and do the things that will result in happy, confident, well-balanced children? Have you ever wondered what makes them so good at it? Now think about the ones you privately don't think are much cop. Why not?

All the best parents I know have one key thing in common. They're relaxed about it. And all the worst ones are hung up on something. Maybe they're not stressed out about how good they are as parents (perhaps they should be) but they're hung up about something that affects their ability to be a really good parent.

I know a couple of parents who are neurotically clean and tidy. Their children have to take their shoes off at the door or the whole world falls apart. Even if the shoes are clean. They get really uptight if their children leave anything out of place or make any kind of a mess (even if it gets cleared up later). It makes it impossible for the kids just to relax and enjoy themselves, in case they get grass stains on their trousers, or knock over the ketchup bottle.

I have another friend who is so obsessively competitive that his children are under huge pressure to win every friendly game they ever play. And one who frets excessively every time her child grazes his knees. I bet you can think of plenty of similar examples among people you know.

The really good parents I've encountered, on the other hand, expect their children to be noisy, messy, bouncy, squabbly, whingy and covered in mud. They take it all in their stride. They know they've got 18 years to turn these small creatures into respectable grown-ups, and they pace themselves. No rush to get them acting like adults – they'll get there in good time.

Between you and me, this Rule gets easier with time, though some people still never master it the way true Rules parents do. It's much harder to relax fully with your first baby than with your last teenager to leave home. With babies, you need to focus on the essentials – a healthy baby that isn't too hungry or too uncomfortable – and don't sweat the rest of it. It doesn't matter if their poppers are done up wrong, or you didn't find time to bath them today, or you've gone away for the weekend without anything for them to sleep in (yes, I have a friend who has done this, and no, she didn't sweat it, being a Rules parent).

Much better altogether if you can get to the end of each day, put your feet up with a glass of wine or a G&T,* and say cheerfully to each other, 'What the hell...they're all still alive so we must have got something right'.

REALLY GOOD PARENTS EXPECT THEIR CHILDREN TO BE NOISY, MESSY, BOUNCY, SQUABBLY, WHINGY AND COVERED IN MUD

---

* No, I'm not encouraging parents to use alcohol to get them through. Just relax!

Be yourself

Isn't it just so tempting to reinvent yourself when you meet somebody new who you really fancy? Or to try and be who you think they are looking for? You could become really sophisticated, or maybe strong and silent and mysterious. At least you could stop embarrassing yourself by making jokes at inappropriate moments, or being pathetic about coping with problems.

Actually, no you couldn't. At least, you might manage it for an evening or two, or even a month or two, but it's going to be tough keeping it up forever. And if you think this person is the one – you know, the one – then you might be spending the next half century or so with them. Just imagine, 50 years of pretending to be sophisticated, or suppressing your natural sense of humour.

That's not going to happen, is it? And would you really want a lifetime of lurking behind some sham personality you've created? Imagine how that would be, unable ever to let on that this wasn't really you at all, for fear of losing them. And suppose they find out in a few weeks' or months' or years' time, when you finally crack? They're not going to be very impressed, and nor would you be if it was them who turned out to have been acting out of character all along.

I'm not saying you shouldn't try to turn over the occasional new leaf; improve yourself a bit. We should all be doing that all the time, and not only in our love life. Sure, you can try to be a bit more organized, or less negative. Changing your behaviour is all fine and good. This Rule is about changing your basic personality. That won't work, and you'll tie yourself in knots trying to do it convincingly.

So be yourself. Might as well get it all out in the open now. And if that's not who they're looking for, at least you won't get in too deep before they find out. And you know what? Maybe they don't actually like sophisticated. Perhaps strong silent types don't do it for them. Maybe they'll love your upfront sense of humour. Perhaps they want to be with someone who needs a bit of looking after.

You see, if you fake it, you'll attract someone who belongs with a person that isn't you. And how will that help? Somewhere out there is someone who wants exactly the kind of person you are, complete with all the flaws and failings you come with. And I'll tell you something else – they won't even see them as flaws and failings. They'll see them as part of your unique charm. And they'll be right.

MIGHT AS WELL GET IT ALL OUT IN THE OPEN NOW